# The Beer Drinker's
# Guide to Munich

# The
# Beer Drinker's Guide
# To Munich

## Larry Hawthorne

**Second Edition**

Freizeit
Publishers

THE BEER DRINKER'S GUIDE TO MUNICH
Copyright © 1991 by Larry Hawthorne
First Printing 1991
Second Printing 1992, revised
Printed in the United States of America

Published by
Freizeit Publishers
377 Keahole Street
Suite 6-265
Honolulu, Hawaii 96825

---

Photos by author and
Friedrich Zenz, pg. 139
Christl Reiter, pg. 143

Illustration by
Heather Hawthorne, pg. 19

Cover:  19th Century woodcut
by Ludwig Richter (1803-1884)

Library of Congress Catalogue Card Number:
92-71254
ISBN: 0-9628555-0-2

*To all those, over the years,*
*who have come to*
*Munich as strangers*
*and left as good friends.*
*Zum Wohl!*

# Contents

*Munich is a kind of German heaven . . . A great Germanic dream translated into life . . . . The best beer in Germany, in the world, is made there, and there are enormous beer cellars that are renowned throughout the land. The Bavarian is the National Good Fellow. He is supposed to be a witty and eccentric creature, and millions of postcards are printed of him in his national costume blowing the froth away from a foaming stein of beer. In other parts of Germany, people will lift their eyes and sigh rapturously when you say you are going to Munich: 'Ach! München . . . is schön!'*

**American Novelist Thomas Wolf**
***The Web and the Rock***

## A Word About the Beer Rating System

Rating schemes are always risky. They pretend to impose my opinion over your own, and that is not the intent. Rather, it is a tool — just a benchmark really — that should save you some time and help you experience and enjoy Munich at its best. My ratings for each establishment employ a 10 point scale, 10 being best, in "half-beer" increments. Thus a 5-beer rating is tops on the list. I'll tell you, picking them isn't easy. It's a lot like judging a beauty pageant when all the contestants are voluptuous vixens. In writing this book and over the years, I have visited literally scores of beer halls and beer gardens. (Literary research is full of personal sacrifices like that.) If they didn't rate at least a five (2-1/2 beers) on my scale of suds, they didn't make the pages of this book. Some are better than others, but be assured that every establishment listed here is worthy of your patronage. I hope you enjoy them as much as I do. Cheers!

## Beer Drinkers only think they're perfect!

Great care was taken to verify the information and assure the accuracy of this guide at the time it went to press. However, along with the inevitable passage of time will come change. The printed page will never keep up with it all and there will always be some errors likely to occur. The price of a beer, opening and closing times, the *ruhetag* "rest day" each week when the establishment is closed are always subject to change. Smart travelers will call and double-check important items before committing to travel. I've tried to give you plenty of phone numbers in case you need them. Hopefully, they won't change. Also, exact dates of Munich's annual events are sometimes locked in only a year in advance. The out-year dates listed in the five-year fest calendar (pg. 145) are probable and could shift slightly, depending on the city's final scheduling. They should be re-confirmed with the Munich visitors bureau prior to traveling.

*The Beer Drinker's Guide to Munich* is constantly being revised and updated. Your own personal experiences in using this book — the good and the bad — can help greatly in confirming or revising the opinions and information in this guide. Send your letters to Freizeit Publishers, 377 Keahole St., Suite 6-265, Honolulu, Hawaii 96825. Thanks, we'd love to hear from you.

# Introduction

*S* itting in the Hirschgarten one balmy summer afternoon a number of years ago, I felt suddenly alone. There must have been the usual 8,000 or so Münchners there that day. When I looked up from my beer and moved my pretzel aside I was struck that in the loud din of conversation not a word of English was spoken. The inescapable conclusion was simple: Visitors from around the world love Munich. They love the food, the beer, the museums, the churches. They are fascinated by the jovial, fun-loving Bavarians and are sure to include Munich on every tour itinerary. But when it comes to a knowledge of the city, they're like Columbus in search of the New World: not sure where they're going, or how to get there. And then they have trouble putting their slides together when they get back because they're not certain where they have been. This guide is an answer to that.

It began on the backs of beer mats and paper napkins as ink-stained directions to a few uncharted beer gardens and beer halls not listed in any of the big travel guides. It later moved to stapled, mimeographed pages handed out to friends who wanted to enjoy Munich the way the locals do but just didn't know where to go or how to get there. When it finally became a book, the natural restrictions of time and writer's cramp had winnowed the field down to just the very best.

The best, as you will see, does not always mean the biggest, or the most famous. But it does mean the ones where the adventurous traveler can expect to find the most fun. It will lead you to those places that, as though some closely guarded state secret, are overlooked by most foreign visitors in Munich.

More than addresses or landmarks on a map, each beer garden, beer hall or beer pub has its own compelling story and colorful history, often closely linked with Munich itself.

I've taken painstaking care to insure that the establishments listed have the welcome mat out. The *wirts* (the proprietors) have assured me personally that they are eager for your business and will show you traditional Bavarian hospitality during your visit. That's why I've written this guide in your interest and not theirs.

There is life after the Hofbräuhaus. You only have to find it!

# Munich's U-Bahn and S-Bahn Public Transport System (MVV)

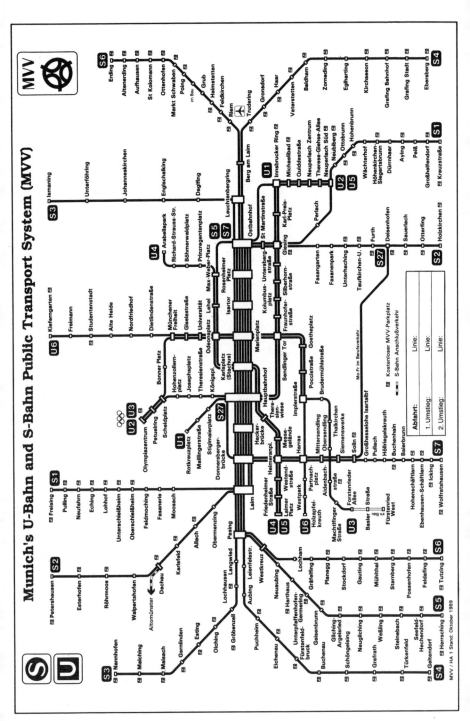

# Getting Around Munich
# With MVV

*N*avigating Munich by private automobile is no way to spend a vacation. City traffic is heavy, it's easy to get lost, there are too many one-way streets to recover quickly, and finding a parking space is a lot like waiting for the leaves to turn. Thankfully, there is an alternative for Munich is blessed with one of the most accessible and efficient public transportation systems in the world. The four-tiered network of subways (U-bahn ), suburban railways (S-bahn ), streetcars, and buses makes getting around a breeze. Here are a few reasons to leave the car at home or parked in one of the city's many in-door parking structures and rely on MVV (*Münchner Verkerhs- und Tarifverbund*) to visit all the beer gardens, beer halls, lokals and restaurants in this book.

❑ **MVV is safe, clean, and fast.** You won't get mugged, you won't get dirty, and you'll get there in a hurry. Simple as that.

❑ **It's dependable.** The trains, trams and buses run on time. Schedules are clearly posted and universally adhered to.

❑ **It's flexible.** There are often several alternative routes to the same destination, with overlapping bus, streetcar or other rail service.

❑ **It's getting better.** The city is continually expanding and improving the system. Outlying areas that were inaccessible just a year or so ago are now easily reached.

❑ **It's incredibly cheap.** With the special all-day group tickets now available, shoe leather is more expensive.

❑ **It's smart.** Using public transportation means full enjoyment of the beer gardens and lokals. No one should get behind the wheel of an automobile even after one beer. It's illegal, it's dumb, and it's unnecessary. A relatively low blood-alcohol level of .08 is the legal limit to operate an automobile in Germany. While German authorities are very tolerant of pedestrians who celebrate too much, they throw the book at anyone who drinks and drives. It means time in jail, a heavy fine, automatic loss of license, and a lot of embarrassment. If this were the only reason to stay with the public transit system, it would be enough.

### 'Wo ist der Hauptbahnhof?'

The concept of this book is simple. Detailed directions to each  beer garden or beer hall begin at the Hauptbahnhof, the main train station. In Munich, like no other German or European town, the central station is the hub of the city's spoked transportation network.   Four underground systems, seven suburban rail lines, and several more bus and tram routes all converge at the Hauptbahnhof. It is the logical and most convenient starting point for any trip within the city or to nearby suburbs. With the Hauptbahnhof as a base, each route is carefully mapped with full graphic and written instructions. In most instances, one or possibly two modes of transportation are required, followed by a short walk (usually only a couple blocks) to the designated establishment. Careful attention should be paid to whether a U- or S-bahn is used. The two train systems are similar in many respects. They are propelled by the same electric engines, they use the same style of passenger cars. In some cases, they traverse similar routes and stop in the same stations. However, the two systems are completely separate and are accessed from different levels. The subterranean U-bahn is usually one level below the S-bahn and services a much smaller area.

## Signing

Munich's stations are filled with clues to help travelers stay on the right track or find the correct exit to the street they need or the next mode of transportation. This is cleverly accomplished through the use of pictures of buses, streetcars, etc., posted in conspicuous places. The Europeans have perfected this system of pictographs to minimize the need for multiple languages. The system is extremely easy to follow without the need to know more than a smattering of German. At transit terminals, such as U- or S-bahn stops, posted signs point the way to nearby street exits and connections for continuing travel.

With just a little practice, one can also interpret the wealth of information available at every boarding point. It usually consists of a posted time schedule, a complete map of the route, a sequential listing of stops and travel times between them, as well as available transfers. As if that weren't enough, on board the train, tram or bus is another easy-to-read annotated map, usually plastered on the ceiling. It provides a running reference of

**Most bus and tram stops have posted information (right) covering routes, schedules and sequence of stops.**

**Signs, like the one below, help travelers find their way. This one in a U-bahn station indicates the stop (Marienplatz) and that S-bahn and bus connections can be made by exiting to the right.**

points along the route. Bus and tram stops are easily identified by the ubiquitous green H on a yellow background. The "H" stands for *haltestelle*, the German word for stop.

## S- and U-bahn Systems

Most subway and suburban railroad systems in the world's major metropolitan areas follow a common code in identifying transit routes and directions. Any frequent urban traveler will recognize Munich's "last-stop" identifier system. Basically, the last stop on any given line will serve as the direction (*richtung* in German) to look for. Thus, if you want to reach Kolumbusplatz from the Hauptbahnhof, you look on the MVV map (printed in this book) and find that two U-bahn lines serve Kolumbusplatz, U-1 and U-2. Either will take you there. However, to make certain you head in the right direction you would take U-1 toward Innsbrucker Ring (last stop in the same direction you're headed) or U-2 toward Neuperlach Süd (last stop on the U-2 line). The last-stop-indicates-direction formula works for every other MVV mode of travel. Occasionally, major intermediate stops are also used to indicate direction — such as "Richtung (direction) Marienplatz" or "Richtung Hauptbahnhof". In suburban areas you will often see "Innenstadt" to indicate the direction of travel is toward the city center (Hauptbahnhof).

Since most U- and S-bahn stations are at major crossroads throughout the city, it isn't unusual to find three or four different exits to choose from. The maps in this book try to anticipate the need to exit the station at the right spot. When a particular exit is required, it is highlighted.

## Tageskarte

There are a number of fare structures, and a variety of tickets offered, but the best deal is so far ahead of the others that it's the only one worth considering. In May 1990, the Munich public transport company took the best of small-group tickets and all-day fares and combined them into one ticket, the Tageskarte. Now, a small group or family can travel most everywhere in Munich, take all four modes of transportation, make as many stops as desired, travel the entire morning, evening, and into the next morning, for the cost of a one-mile taxi ride, or currently DM 8.

The Tageskarte, or day ticket, is good anywhere within the 20-kilometer diameter area shown in light blue on the city's transportation maps. The *blaue zone* or MVV Innenraum encompasses the bet-

**One of the best deals in Munich, the Tageskarte can be obtained from ticket machines that display this notice.**

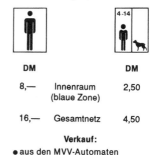

# Tageskarte

Vor Fahrtantritt entwerten.
Gültig für beliebig viele Fahrten bis 4 Uhr des folgenden Tages für eine Person.

Eine Tageskarte für Erwachsene gilt montags bis freitags ab 9.00 Uhr sowie an Samstagen, Sonntagen und Feiertagen ganztägig für 5 Personen (davon höchstens zwei Personen ab dem vollendeten 18. Lebensjahr) und 1 Hund.

| DM | | DM |
|---|---|---|
| 8,— | Innenraum (blaue Zone) | 2,50 |
| 16,— | Gesamtnetz | 4,50 |

**Verkauf:**
- aus den MVV-Automaten
- an der Verkaufsstelle

ter part of the city. For example, only two beer gardens in this book (Kloster Andechs and Weihenstephen) are beyond the zone. All others are within easy reach with a Tageskarte. The time element of the ticket is unlimited travel (within the zone) Monday through Friday, from 9 a.m. to 4 a.m. the next morning (note: a little academic since most lines stop running around 1 a.m.). On Saturdays, Sundays and holidays, the 9 a.m. restriction is waived and the ticket can be used as early as desired. The group aspect of the ticket covers up to five persons (related or not), only two of whom may be 18 or over, and one dog (!). Thus, you and a friend, or a spouse and your three kids, or somebody's kids, plus a stray dog can ride the rails all day long for around the cost of a beer where you're headed. There is also a children's Tageskarte available, in the event a child (4-14 years old) is traveling alone or your group exceeds the three-kid limit. An "all-zones" Tageskarte that offers essentially the same deal but is good anywhere MVV has service, sells for double the price.

It's hard to imagine any better transportation bargain than the Tageskarte. The pass can be bought through vending machines at most stations or ticket counters. It is also available at reception desks in many hotels, tourist bureaus and city information offices, and a number of Munich's shops and department stores. The ticket is good as soon as validated in one of the blue time-and-date clock machines (they have a large "E" on their face) at the entrance to U- and S-bahn tracks, and at bus and tram stops . (Note: At bus and trams stops, you should validate tickets before you board. Most on-board validating machines are not yet set up for the Tageskarte.)

Once you've validated the ticket and are on board, you may be struck by the fact that nobody seems to want to check it. The honor system is in force in Germany and is seldom violated. Verification of tickets is infrequent and you may ride for days without being checked. When a "kontrol" is made, however, those who can't produce a validated ticket are looking at a stiff on-the-spot DM 60 fine and a lot of embarrassment in a crowded car filled with paying customers. Buy the Tageskarte, stamp it, and then forget about it.

Munich City Districts

2 Altstadt, Zentrum, Theresienhöhe, Westend, Untersendling
5 Zentrum Süd, Gärtnerplatz, Balde-platz, Deutsches Museum
19 Neuhausen, Gern, Nymphenburg
21 Laim, Blumenau, Kleinhadern
22 Zentrum, Ost, Lehel
40 Schwabing, Englischer Garten
45 Freimann, Neuherberg
50 Moosach
60 Pasing, Obermenzing, Neuaubing
70 Sendling, Thalkirchen, Hadern, Waldfriedhof
71 Solln, Fürstenried, Forstenried
80 Haidhausen, Bogenhausen, Steinhausen, Berg am Laim, Ramersdorf
81 Bogenhausen, Oberföhring
82 Tudering, Gartenstadt, Waldtrudering, Riem
83 Perlach, Neuperlach
90 Giesing, Harlaching, Fasangarten

# Beer Drinker's Etiquette

*M* aybe not manners, that would be going too far. Yet there are certain customs, traditions and standards of acceptable behavior that prevail in most Munich beer establishments. Here are a few of the most notable ones that may save the first-time visitor some unnecessary embarrassment.

### Table Ownership

The notion of table ownership has been modified in Munich's crowded beer establishments. In fact, reservations are seldom taken and available seats are usually fair game, on a first-come-serve basis. Thus, new arrivals are welcome to join occupied tables where there are empty chairs by inquiring politely if the seat is "noch frei". Also, there is no obligation to carry on conversations with new-found table partners although after a couple beers it's a golden opportunity to break the ice. Chances are they're tourists, just like you.

### The Stammtisch

An exception to the above is the *Stammtisch*. Clearly marked, usually with a sign or wrought-iron work, the Stammtisch is reserved for regulars. By definition, you are not a regular. Every beer hall and most beer gardens have one or two of these specially reserved tables. Even established patrons will assume nothing for granted and usually knock politely on the table as if to gain permission from the other Stammtisch regulars before sitting down. If you sit at a Stammtisch by mistake (it's easy to do since it's often the only table with any available seating) you'll soon know it. Others at the table will consider it their duty to instruct you in this quaint custom. Usually they do this by treating you as though you have a social disease. If you're so unlucky to sit in a particular favorite chair of an arriving regular he may sit in your lap. Again, look for the signs or be prepared to spend the evening talking war stories from a completely new point of view.

## Self-Service or Not

If no one seems to want to wait on you, and you are not broken out in some form of skin rash, see if your table has a table cloth. If none, you may be sitting at a *selbstbedienung* (self-service) table where you will be expected to fend for yourself in securing your own beer and food. The roots of this custom go back several hundred years and are usually enforced in beer gardens more than in beer halls. It seems that during the time of King Ludwig I, Munich's brew masters decided it would be a good idea to branch out. Instead of just selling their beer at indoor *bräustuben* they beseeched the monarch to allow them to establish outdoor gardens or *bierkellers*. (When you see the term "keller", by the way, it usually refers to the cellar where the beer is kept cool and not where it is dispensed. Thus bierkellers are in reality beer gardens.) The king agreed to the idea and soon beer barons all over Munich were reaping huge profits through skyrocketing sales of their foamy product. In time, the poorer citizenry of Munich found that it was cheaper to bring their own lunch to picnic under the flourishing chestnut trees. Again, sensing a disappearing market, the beer-hall-now-garden proprietors petitioned their king to let them ban this practice that was cutting into their margins. In one of Munich's great compromises the king decreed brown-baggers would still be allowed, but only at tables without table cloths. That unwritten law exists today. Most beer gardens allow patrons to bring their own food but they must be content to sit at uncovered tables (resourceful Münchners bring their own table cloths).

In some of the more traditional beer gardens, you will be required — if opting to take the self-service route — to select your own liter glass mug from a wooden rack, wash it and then dutifully take it to the nearest *bier ausschank* to be filled. The Hirschgarten is the most obvious example of this still-surviving custom.

## Paying the Bill and Tipping

A favorite and telling cartoon has a typical restaurant patron clutching desperately at the leg of a smug waiter with one hand, a fist full of money in the other, in a futile attempt to pay his check. Like most caricatures, it exaggerates. But not much. For some reason, attracting the attention of a waiter in time to settle the bill invites the supreme effort. You announce your intentions by saying "zahlen, bitte." (Check, please.) Herr Ober will invariably answer with "sofort!", which loosely translated means "right away." Don't you believe it. "Sofort" sounds a lot like "go for it!" and that would be more to the point. Be patient.

If just ordering drinks, be prepared to pay when served. If you order food along with beverages, the waiter or waitress will usually run a tab and present you with a check when you are ready to leave.

Tipping is a relatively recent innovation in Germany. Thanks to the post-war armies of invading tourists, the custom has caught on, sort of.

Restaurant and beer hall proprietors have accommodated these compulsive gratuity donors by including a 12-15 percent "service" charge in the price of every item on the menu—beer, food, everything. The tip is now conveniently included, but unfortunately has little or no influence on the quality of the service. It's just there, and it's already added in when you pick up the check. Rounding up to the next mark is the custom most Germans follow, although many will still pay the bill to the exact pfennig without losing any sleep over it. What works for Münchners should work for you, too. An exception is taxis, where the driver expects a 10-15 percent tip.

### Odds and Ends

When ordering from the menu, make sure all in your party know what they want. If anyone falters, the waiter will skip you and come back when all minds are made up, say in a half-hour or so. Don't be afraid to point, or order by the number. They're used to it.

Those neat, liter glass mugs may make great souvenirs but there are guards at the door just waiting to nab anyone trying to liberate one. You can buy them in the gift shop or at the souvenir stand.

In an odd reversal of customs, the beer halls are closing when the lights are dimmed; open when the lights are at full blast.

Men, don't be shocked to find cleaning women permanently stationed in the restrooms. You'll get used to it, and they're usually more interested in reading their book. If you wash your hands and use a paper towel (and we hope you do) throw a couple 10 pfennig pieces on the plate. For women, the usual toilet fee is 50 pfennig. I don't know why it costs more.

If you know some German, try it. It's appreciated. On the same hand, don't expect everyone to know English. They won't.

If you can't meet the requirement to order a full liter of regular beer, you can side-step the provision by ordering a *Weizen*, or wheat beer. This style of beer always comes in a tall, half-liter, wide-mouthed glass.

Above all, remember that fun is tolerated and encouraged, public drunkenness is not.

**The proper
way to handle
a liter Maß
of beer.**

# Altes Hacker–haus

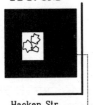

Dult Str.

Hacken Str.

Hermann Sack Str.

St. Nos.

Sendlinger Str.

St. Nos.

U–Bahn
Sendlinger Tor

Hauptbahnhof
  U–Bahn 1 or 2
  to Sendlinger Tor
Sendlinger Tor
  Walk up Sendlinger
  Str. as shown
  on map (note street
  addresses ascend on
  one side of street,
  descend on the
  other).

 Altes Hackerhaus
Sendlinger Strasse 75
8000 Munich 2

 (089) 2605026

 Hacker–Pschorr Brau

9 a.m. to 12 midnight

 180 in Beer Garden
250 in Restaurant

# Altes Hackerhaus

*A*ny Munich establishment with "altes" or "old" in its name ought to have a deep appreciation of its past. Altes Hackerhaus certainly has that. In fact, a room of this ancient edifice is dedicated to the memory, the life and times of one of the city's oldest brewing families, Hacker-Pschorr. An entire wall is taken up with a mural depicting the historic family tree.

There's hardly room to depict the full story of this traditional Bavarian restaurant and beer garden. It must have been a welcome sight to thirsty travelers arriving at Munich's back door in 1738 when Brewer Simon Hacker (thus "Hacker-Brau") decided to post his menu. Just inside Munich's southern gate, Sendlinger Tor, the offering included fresh beer brewed on the premises, and a growing list of late-Renaissance munchies that would have oiled the sandals of any wayfaring stranger.

A Hacker daughter, Therese, expanded the family business by marrying one Josef Pschorr in 1793 (thus "Hacker-Pschorr-Brau"). The ancestral digs handed down among the Hackers and Pschorrs, father to son, uncle to nephew, blossomed and the centralized beer outlet remained a Munich fixture for another quarter century. In 1825, the brewery portion burnt to the ground, but the family living quarters survived, though badly damaged. By 1831, the house was completely rebuilt. Beer was brewed elsewhere, and the *brauhaus* continued operation, in much the same manner as today.

Altes Hackerhaus is on Sendlinger Strasse, about midway between Sendlinger Tor and the Neues Rathaus (the one with the Glockenspiel). The street is numbered in the old style — an attempt to confuse invading armies? — with addresses rising on one side, descending on the other. Munich's own version of Fleet Street, the Sendlinger Strasse also houses the editorial headquarters of most of the city's major newspapers. Inside the restaurant's vaulted-arch corridors, journalists rub elbows and exchange *Prosits* (toasts) with well-heeled Münchners who frequent the district's nearby jewelry shops and expensive chic haberdasheries (used Levi jackets at $150 a pop!).

Altes Hackerhaus is a local refuge of sorts, with lots of old-timey atmosphere, reasonable prices and a small but comfortable courtyard beer garden. This is a place to relax and enjoy a good meal, in a convenient location that is just around the corner from the Marienplatz and Munich's main pedestrian zone. It earns highest marks for traditional Bavarian eats and a quiet setting amid the hub-bub of one of the town's busier commercial areas. Maybe not a full day venue, but definitely worth a visit, especially during a leisurely walk through Munich's historic quarter. It gets 2-1/2 beers.

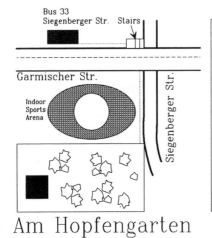

Bus 33
Siegenberger Str.   Stairs

Garmischer Str.

Siegenberger Str.

Indoor
Sports
Arena

Hauptbahnhof
  U-Bahn 4 or 5
  to Heimeranplatz
Heimeranplatz
  Exit to Bus 33;
  take Bus 33 to
  Siegenberger Str.
Siegenberger Str.
  From bus stop,
  walk down stairs to
  Siegenberger Str.,
  past sports arena
  to beer garden.

# Am Hopfengarten

Am Hopfengarten
Siegenburger Strasse 43
8000 Munich 70

(089) 7608846

Lowenbrau

10 a.m. to 10 p.m.

1200 in Beer Garden

# Am Hopfengarten

*I*n West Park's eastern fringe, across the street from a strip of well-tended *gärtenplätze* (private garden plots) is Am Hopfengarten. Incongruously located in the shadow of the city's large indoor sports arena, the beer garden is an unexpected addition to what is otherwise a contrived setting of manicured, mounded turfed areas and man-made lakes.

The beer garden sports a self-service fast-food (*schmankerl*) stand whose speciality — in addition to good Löwenbräu beer — is some of the meatiest spare-ribs this side of a Texas barbecue.

Shade is at a premium here, since the usual stand of chestnut trees is, by definition, only as old as the park itself is new (developed for the International Botanical Exhibit of 1983). Still, the *wirt* (owner) has taken some care in providing an inviting atmosphere for guests and an especially attractive children's play area. The smoothed brick climbing structure is contained within a sandbox that should keep the kiddies entertained for hours. All the more lucrative for the grown-ups to enjoy a relaxing day with a cold *Maß* (liter mug) of Munich's most prolific beer and some of the best take-out food in town.

Am Hopfengarten is average by Munich's high standards for such beer-dispensing emporia, but worth a look-see nevertheless. It earns 2-1/2 beers.

Am Hopfengarten's fast-food stand is a major attraction of this West Park beer garden.

23

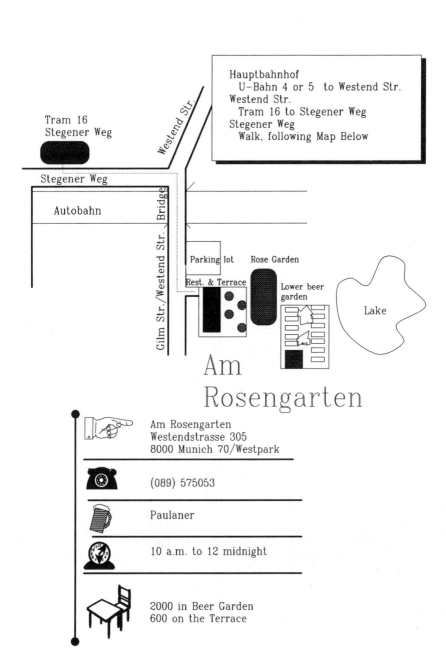

Hauptbahnhof
   U-Bahn 4 or 5  to Westend Str.
Westend Str.
   Tram 16 to Stegener Weg
Stegener Weg
   Walk, following Map Below

Tram 16
Stegener Weg

Westend Str.

Stegener Weg

Autobahn

Bridge

Gilm Str./Westend Str.

Parking lot    Rose Garden

Rest. & Terrace

Lower beer
garden

Lake

Am
Rosengarten

Am Rosengarten
Westendstrasse 305
8000 Munich 70/Westpark

(089) 575053

Paulaner

10 a.m. to 12 midnight

2000 in Beer Garden
600 on the Terrace

# Am Rosengarten

*A*m Rosengarten is a little schizophrenic, in a nice sort of way. It may all have been the result of the 1983 International Botanical Exhibition, which really gave this place its start. One can imagine a convention of thirsty horticultural designers descending on Munich's spacious West Park with a truckload of bulbs and several kegs of beer. "OK, let's put the rose garden here, right next to the lake," must have been the plan. "Now, where to put the beer?"

The answer became Am Rosengarten, a two-tiered beer garden with a little something for everybody. The upper restaurant has a terrace designed in triangular red brick. Lots of umbrellas provide the shade over a series of bedecked tables serviced by bow-tied waiters. The glass-enclosed restaurant itself is decorated in a modern, somewhat sterile varnished wood style. The food is hearty, although a little expensive, and the ambience invites more the "Kaffee and Küchen Klatch" folks than the down-and-dirty suds for lunch bunch.

No matter. Just below the terraced haute cuisine centrum, and a (no foolin') rose garden with a reported 100 varieties of living corsages, is a neat, clean and exceedingly welcome beer garden in the traditional mode (even a May pole). Benches and tables under the mandatory stand of chestnut trees mark this analgesic annex. There's a beer and *schmankerl* outlet, manned by folks wearing Levis, where you can help yourself to brew by the liter, smoked fish on a stick, and Bavarian delicacies by the paper-plateload. Predictably, the prices are more conventional and the gastronomic fare no less filling.

With less than a decade behind it, Am Rosengarten is still a mite undergrown in terms of its natural shade-bearing flora. A few more rough edges and a few less gardeners would also serve well here. The well-manicured look is fine for the local arboretum, but beer gardens deserve more grass and less class.

Still, Am Rosengarten is a fine place to while away the afternoon. The view may be a little fabricated (does the lake really have a plastic bottom?) but impressive, nevertheless. Here's a place where you can enthrall your date with your adroit handling of the terrace wine list, then retire to the more sympathetic beer garden for some real fun.

Freedom of choice is worth something. The dual-faceted Am Rosengarten earns 3-1/2 beers.

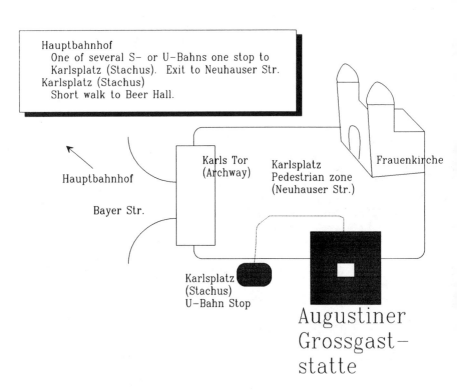

Hauptbahnhof
    One of several S- or U-Bahns one stop to
    Karlsplatz (Stachus).  Exit to Neuhauser Str.
Karlsplatz (Stachus)
    Short walk to Beer Hall.

Hauptbahnhof

Bayer Str.

Karls Tor
(Archway)

Karlsplatz
Pedestrian zone
(Neuhauser Str.)

Frauenkirche

Karlsplatz
(Stachus)
U-Bahn Stop

Augustiner
Grossgast-
statte

Augustiner Grossgaststatte
Neuhauserstrasse 16
8000 Munich 2/Altstadt

(089) 5519901

Augustiner Edelstoff

9 a.m. to 12 midnight

250 in Beer Garden
1500 in Restaurant
    and Beer Hall

# Augustiner Großgaststätte

*Y*ou'll fall in love with this place faster than you can say Augustiner Großgaststätte (Ah-Gus-Teener Grose-Gahst-State-uh). Munich beer halls aren't big on easy name recognition. Not that it mattered much when this establishment was founded in 1328. The Augustin Brothers were not exactly dealing in heavy intellectual challenges back then. Their mental gymnastics were limited to the opening stanza of early morning prayers and remembering the four main ingredients — hops, barley, yeast and water — of the beer they brewed.

Eventually, secular entrepreneurship won out over clerical enterprise, and the State of Bavaria took over the brewing art from the heavenly brethren. (Anything you can brew, we can brew better!) Up until 1885, the beer that many still consider the best in Munich was produced on site. The brewery was later moved to its current location on Landsberger Straße, but the *Gasthaus* remained.

Augustiner Großgaststätte, essentially a traditional beer hall with a

**Augustiner Großgaststätte around 1890. A liter of beer cost 26 pfennigs.**

small beer garden, is today a veritable in-door beer oasis, smack dab in the middle of Munich's pedestrian zone. The Gothic-arched ceilings and fresco-painted walls promote a medieval, "cloistered" environment. The scenes portray the brethren at their best, totally immersed in a centuries-old quest for the quintessential brew. The interior is reminiscent of the better-known Hofbräuhaus without the raucous atmosphere, for better or worse, depending on the mood of the moment.

The restaurant and beer hall serve up excellent food, with roasted pork knuckles and white sausages as menu mainstays. Still, the sweet, aromatic and liberally dispensed Augustiner beer is the liquid hallmark of this establishment. Half-liters are readily available, thus eliminating the usual investment in time and saturability demanded by nearby competitors.

The relatively small, courtyard beer garden, more a filtered place in the sun, is refuge from the smoke-filled cavernous rooms of the beer hall. Yet, its Italian rococo styling and historic value as the original cloister garden make it a favorite among beer aficionados who know their way around Munich.

Augustiner Großgaststätte is a lot of the old world with a bit of the new. There is no more traditional a beer hall in all of Munich. The *gemütlichkeit* index is high, garnering this living historical monument a rating of four full and frothy beers.

**The afternoon sun casts long shadows on Karlsplatz, vicinity of Augustiner Großgaststätte.**

Summertime crowds enjoy outside dining at Augustiner Großgaststätte.

# Augustiner Keller

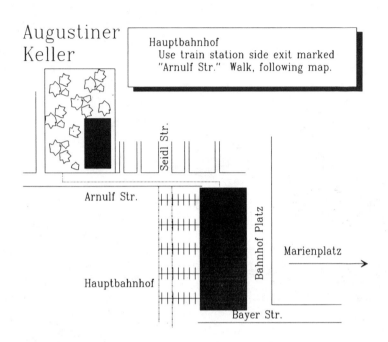

Hauptbahnhof
    Use train station side exit marked
    "Arnulf Str."  Walk, following map.

Seidl Str.

Arnulf Str.

Bahnhof Platz

Marienplatz

Hauptbahnhof

Bayer Str.

Augustiner Keller
Arnulfstrasse 52
8000 Munich 2

(089) 594393

Augustiner Edelstoff

10 a.m. to 12 midnight

5000 in Beer Garden
200 in Restaurant
500 in Ballroom

# *Augustiner Keller*

*W*hat if you could enjoy Munich's best-tasting beer, served in its most famous, historic and attractive beer garden? And what if you could reach such an inviting place in less than 10 minutes by foot from the Hauptbahnhof? You can. Just take the Arnulf Str. exit from the main train station and walk the several blocks to Augustiner Keller. No one should visit Munich, even for a day, and miss this wonderful beer garden experience.

Augustiner is a spacious setting, amid centuries-old chestnut trees, seemingly spread over several country acres. On a warm summer day, 5,000 seats are hardly enough to accommodate the hordes of Germans who congregate here. The *stammtisches* are often filled with high-ranking political figures and the most famous names of Germany's entertainment industry (Bavarian Radio and TV network headquarters nearby). There's still plenty of room for "common folk", though, and Augustiner is a great equalizer among the classes of this Bavarian capital, where blue, white and embroidered native garb collars match beer for beer, elbow to elbow. Unlike other beer gardens which tend to empty out soon after dark, Augustiner maintains its high level late into the evening. The final table of customers

"Bier Ochse" were used during the 19th century to retrieve heavy kegs of beer from Augustiner's cellar cooling vaults.

will grudgingly depart only after "last call", fast on the heels of midnight.

The keller alludes to decades past, before refrigeration, when wooden kegs of brew were kept in the cellar to retain the freshness and cool temperature of their liquid contents. Aptly named "beer oxen" were employed to turn the wheel of a leveraged pulley system that would raise the casks from their subterranean storage to allow gravity fed distribution of the beer to thirsty customers in the Augustiner garden. The last bovine beer caddy was given his retirement papers in 1891, replaced by a more efficient *deus ex machina* born of the Industrial Revolution.

Previously, the business had been in the hands of a family of book publishers, thus the name Büchlbräukeller until 1848 when it was sold to Gabriel Sedlmayr, patriarch of the Spaten brewing chain. Ol' Gabe didn't hold onto it long, though, and in 1862, Augustiner Brewery under the proprietorship of Joseph Wagner took over. It has remained a purveyor of the label ever since. Wagner was instrumental in expanding the garden portion of the property by incorporating a nearby meadow.

Augustiner Keller's reputation as foremost among Munich's beer establishments is well deserved. The mix of table- and self-service beer and food stands offers its diverse group of customers a choice of fare. The service is polite and efficient, probably owing to the relative high-brow clientele ("was that the Bavarian interior minister I just spilled a Maß of beer on!") and the paucity of transient trade. People who come to Augustiner, come back for refills.

Additionally, the restaurant, although dwarfed by the sheer magnitude of the beer garden, could easily stand on its own. It offers full meals in the best Bavarian culinary tradition. On special occasions such as Fasching and Starkbier fests, the interior *Große Festsaal* is employed to host industrial-strength beer bashes. There is even a large children's play area in one section of the beer garden, slightly elevated and blessedly removed from the mainstream of activity.

If there is any negative aspect, it is due to the popularity of this remarkable beer garden: when the weather is good, the seats are as hard to find as a downtown Munich parking place. Worth the gamble, though. Augustiner Keller is a full keg of enjoyment, with a maximum 5 beer rating.

A *Kellnerin* totes a *Maß* of Munich's favorite beer, Augustiner Edelstof (left).

Not far from the Hauptbahnhof and next door to Bavarian television and radio network headquarters, Augustiner Keller (below) attracts large crowds and a middle- to upper-class clientele.

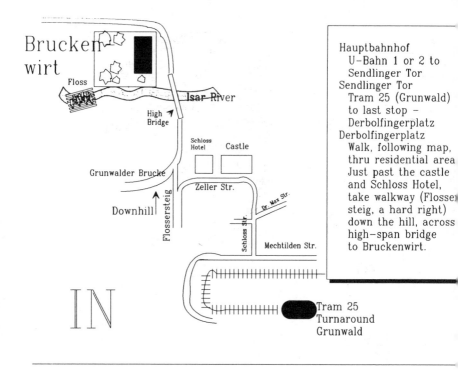

Brucken wirt

Floss

Isar River

High Bridge

Schloss Hotel    Castle

Grunwalder Brucke

Zeller Str.

Dr. Max Str.

Downhill

Flossersteig

Schloss Str.

Mechtilden Str.

IN

Tram 25
Turnaround
Grunwald

Hauptbahnhof
  U-Bahn 1 or 2 to
  Sendlinger Tor
Sendlinger Tor
  Tram 25 (Grunwald)
  to last stop –
  Derbolfingerplatz
Derbolfingerplatz
  Walk, following map,
  thru residential area
  Just past the castle
  and Schloss Hotel,
  take walkway (Flosse
  steig, a hard right)
  down the hill, across
  high–span bridge
  to Bruckenwirt.

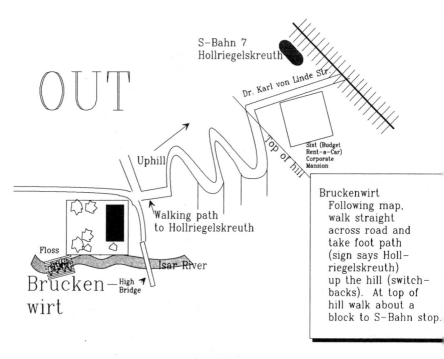

OUT

S-Bahn 7
Hollriegelskreuth

Dr. Karl von Linde Str.

Top of hill

Uphill

Sixt (Budget
Rent-a-Car)
Corporate
Mansion

Walking path
to Hollriegelskreuth

Floss

Isar River

Brucken-  High
wirt     Bridge

Bruckenwirt
  Following map,
  walk straight
  across road and
  take foot path
  (sign says Holl-
  riegelskreuth)
  up the hill (switch-
  backs). At top of
  hill walk about a
  block to S-Bahn stop.

# Brückenwirt

*W*e're going on a field trip, boys and girls. Just a little *ausflug* in the country. And, we'll not retrace our steps along the way. The proprietors of Brückenwirt, literally an anchoring end of the high-span Grunwalder Bridge over the Isar River, are quick to note the variety of means its customers employ to get there. Boat, raft, canoe, swim. (Yeah, you can actually take a dip at this upstream, clear-water point.) On the other hand, you can also take a tram or an S-bahn, and the maps on the opposite page portray two routes, in and out. The in route, arriving by tram, winds by a medieval castle* (complete with moat) and then down the hill and across the bridge to the restaurant and beer garden. The out alternative is a route that winds uphill through a forested area, leading to an S-bahn stop with a direct connection back to the city center. Getting to and fro is literally half the fun.

*The adjacent Schloß Hotel has a 200-seat beer garden of its own.

The trip is longer than most, and about a 20-minute walk each way. But the destination is well worth it, along with an outstanding menu and the usual Maß of beer in the garden. Brückenwirt offers our fieldtrip class a chance to learn about the uniquely Bavarian art of *Flöß* (pronounced "flohes", not "flob"), or Party Rafting.

Now, Bavarians are well-known for their ability to mix business with pleasure. Such was the case a couple centuries ago when loggers in the upper reaches of the Isar would cut their lumber and float it down the river in make-shift rafts to the inhabited regions below. After a hard day on the wooded slopes, the *lederhosen*-clad lumber jacks would see their product safely to market accompanied by a little celebration, a round of song and a great deal of beer. The cruise down the slow-flowing Isar took four to six hours to the nearest waiting mills. That left plenty of time for song and brew, and a tradition was born.

Bruckenwirt
An der Grunwalder Brucke 1
8023 Hollriegelskreuth

(089) 7930167

Lowenbrau

10 a.m. to 12 midnight
Closed on Tuesdays

800 in Beer Garden
100 in Restaurant
300 in Banquet Hall

Eventually, the lumber was more efficiently hauled by truck. So much for the work, but why give up the fun? Flöß is alive and well. Seated in the riverside beer garden at Brückenwirt, one can gain a first-hand glimpse of this venerable local custom. The first clue is the distant sound of an "oompah band" playing traditional Bavarian *Blasmusik*. Eventually a fully laden party raft floats into view, with about 60 revelers, each with a raised mug of foamy beer poised in full *prosit*. Toasts are exchanged with the envious observers along the shore, and as quickly as it came it has floated by. That is, until the next raft 10 minutes later.

Brückenwirt is one of the rare locations to view and enjoy this festive scene. (See Gasthaus Hinterbrühl, another.) It is probably the most rural lokal and beer garden presented here. Yet, it is relatively easy to get to. The scenic mix of pine and chestnut trees give one the feeling of being literally out in the woods. For those who enjoy a walk in the outback, a network of hiking trails—mostly running along the river—is nearby.

Brückenwirt is a combination of scenic enjoyment, fine food and beer, and the opportunity to experience an unusual and invigorating local ritual. Added together, they give this fieldtrip destination a 4-1/2 beer rating.

Note: The Flöß season runs generally from the first of May through the middle of September. Those tempted to jump in and swim out to where the fun is can stay dry and book passage on a Flöß through several companies who provide the service:

| | |
|---|---|
| Josef Seitner Flößbetrieb | Tel. 081-7178518 |
| Angermeier, Gaißach | Tel. 080-428255 |
| Felicitas Beck | Tel. 081-653838 |

**Brückenwirt, on the banks of the Isar River**

36

A woodcut from 1885 portrays the centuries-old tradition of Floß.

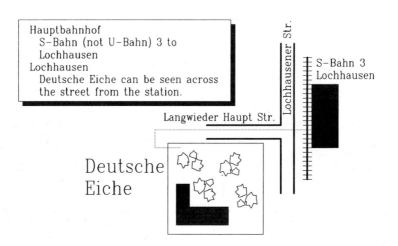

Hauptbahnhof
  S-Bahn (not U-Bahn) 3 to
  Lochhausen
Lochhausen
  Deutsche Eiche can be seen across
  the street from the station.

Lochhausener Str.

S-Bahn 3
Lochhausen

Langwieder Haupt Str.

Deutsche
Eiche

Deutsche Eiche
Ranertstrasse 1
8000 Munich 60

(089) 8141557

Maisacher Brau

9 a.m. to 12 midnight
Closed on Tuesdays

1000 in Beer Garden
260 in Restaurant

# Deutsche Eiche

*D*eutsche Eiche is an impression of old Munich, when the local restaurant and beer garden were an institution alongside the country church and corner train station. This was a place to meet and while away a quiet Sunday afternoon among friends and family. Cares were few, worries better left to those city dwellers down the road.

Life was simple in 1899 when the house on Lochhausen's Ranertstrasse opened its doors and began trading in the gastronomical arts. Deutsche Eiche retains much of that old country charm. The story of this traditional farmhouse turned beer garden revolves around the Mahl and Reisländer families who have managed the business since its inception. Martin and Theresa Mahl were first on the scene at the turn of the century, offering home-cooked meals and cellar-chilled brew. They built a loyal patronage over the next two decades. In 1923, the childless couple turned the business over to their niece Rosa, who had recently married Johann Reisländer upon his return from serving in the Kaiser's Imperial Guard in World War I. The Reisländers and their married daughters have carried forward the family tradition until today.

At a time when large, faceless corporations are snapping up beer gardens by the case, Deutsche Eiche is a rare and pleasant anachronism, a nostalgic hold-over from a bygone era. Pride and quality remain trademarks of this establishment: excellent service, superb cuisine and ever-fresh, chilled Maisacher beer.

Lochhausen, a rural farm village when Deutsche Eiche got its start, is today a Munich suburb. Yet, the annexation is in name only. The village — it remains that — is a world apart from the bustle of the Munich metro-center. Deutsche Eiche is in harmony with this slower-paced way of life. The relaxed atmosphere and unruffled setting is a soothing time-out from the more exciting alternatives offered in the inner city. It's a family affair, and a lot like being invited home for dinner. Certainly well worth the S-Bahn ride to take in a visit.

Deutsche Eiche gets its highest marks for being laid back and tranquil. Comparisons are always difficult, yet sheer enjoyment remains the common denominator that earns Deutsche Eiche a 3-1/2 beer rating.

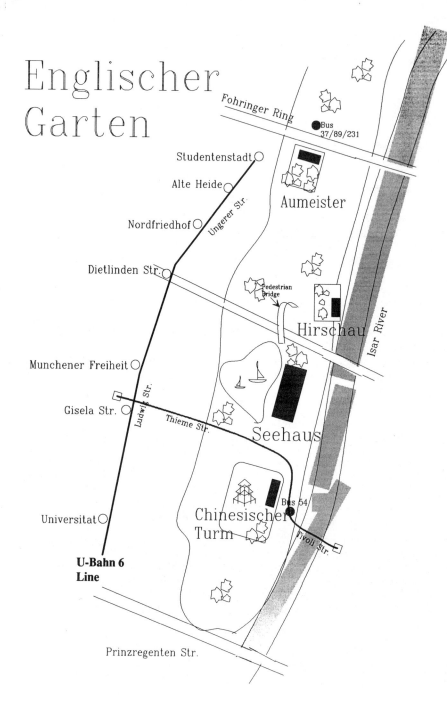

# Englischer Garten

Fohringer Ring

Bus 37/89/231

Studentenstadt

Alte Heide

Ungerer Str.

Aumeister

Nordfriedhof

Dietlinden Str.

Pedestrian Bridge

Hirschau

Isar River

Munchener Freiheit

Ludwig Str.

Gisela Str.

Thieme Str.

Seehaus

Universitat

Bus 54

Chinesischer Turm

Tivoli Str.

**U-Bahn 6 Line**

Prinzregenten Str.

# Englischer Garten
## Four of Munich's Finest

*T*hanks to a transplanted American count, Münchners today enjoy one of the most pleasing central parks in any metropolitan area in the world. The Englischer Garten is a haven for the young and the young at heart. It's a place where strollers mingle unabashedly with nude sunbathers, bicyclists cruise along lakes where non-powered boaters ply their oars through crystal clear waters. Families pack their lunches and spread blankets over lush green lawns amid rolling hills and dales. And, when the weather is best, they all congregate together in one of Englischer Garten's four beer gardens: Chinesicher Turm (Chinese Tower), Seehaus, Hirschau, and Aumeister. They are presented here in logical order, like a walk in the park.

First, though, some history on the Englischer Garten. The park began as a compromise, a royal bribe from Karl Theodor to a rebellious Munich populace. Due to gross mismanagement on his part, the Wittelsbach monarch was faced with a poor wheat harvest and subsequent widespread starvation that threatened his overthrow in 1789. Seeking to avoid the fate of a contemporary royal peer, King Louis XVI, forced to flee his palace that same year during the bloody French Revolution, Karl Theodor relied on the aid of a foreigner, Benjamin Thompson. Thompson was an American without portfolio who sided with the British during his own country's revolution of a decade earlier. Despite questionable loyalties, he was nevertheless awarded the title Count von Rumford and commissioned to do something, anything that might quiet the tumultuous Bavarians.

Demonstrating some of that Yankee ingenuity that had served him well in avoiding being hanged as a traitor in Concord, New Hampshire, Rumford set up soup kitchens and welfare programs that muted the aspiring expectations of the local populace, at least temporarily. As a culminating gesture, he convinced Karl Theodor to set aside a large chunk of his game preserves and a swamp along the Isar on the outskirts of Munich. The whole real estate package was to be developed into a huge public park. The land was drained in order to support something more than just water sports, and the park was laid out in the natural English style, rather than the French neatly manicured mode (anything to avoid inviting comparisons to what was going on in Paris at the time).

Englischer Garten was officially dedicated in 1792 and Rumford and his park were an immediate success. They even named a potato and barley soup after him (cleverly, *Rumfordsuppe*). Still, one is left to only wonder, had Rumford backed a winning horse, would it not be the Amerikanischer Garten today.

The park is three miles long, and a little over a half-mile wide in parts. In addition to being bordered on one side by the Isar River, it has three streams flowing through it. There is a Japanese Teahouse in the southern section. In the central region of the park is a Chinese Pagoda, dating from 1790, which serves as a backdrop to Chinesischer Turm beer garden. Nearby is Kleinhesseloh Lake, a venue for paddle boating and also the setting for Seehaus restaurant and beer garden. Just behind Seehaus is a pedestrian bridge over Diatlinden Strasse, connecting the northern section. The path at the base of the bridge curves around to the right to Hirschau restaurant and beer garden. Walking along further leads to the northern most beer garden, Aumeister, just below Föhringer Ring.

As the map shows, each beer garden can be accessed by U-bahn and a short walk through the park. Better, though, would be to make a day of it and take a stroll through this naturalist's paradise, pausing for a cool one at each stop along the way.

**Chinesischer Turm beer garden in the English Garden.**

# Chinesischer Turm

## in Englischer Garten

*W*ild and crazy people show up at the Chinesischer Turm. "Normal" folk too. Fire-red spiked punk hairdos compete with the Yuppie clean-cut brief-cased look at this massive beer garden (7,000 seats), second only to the Hirschgarten as Munich's largest. Anything and everything is in season. The atmosphere is as informal as a Saturday morning laundromat, with shorts, tank-tops, barefoot or sandals as the preferred apparel. In fact, a few local patrons may seem to have left their clothes still in the dryer. Nude bathing "beaches" are just a couple hundred yards away.

Chinesischer Turm is the watering hole of choice for most of Munich's student crowd, but by no means their sole monopoly. The democratic beer garden caters to all walks, all ages, and all circumstances. Everyone is welcome here. The whole affair fronts on a very real looking multi-tiered Chinese wooden pagoda (the stage for Bavarian brass bands on Sunday afternoons). The structure's incongruity with the popular image of the traditional Munich beer garden dissipates quickly with a casual review of the attending clientele. As though it really mattered. The place is fun.

A nearby restaurant offers table service and blue-plate specials. It loses out though to competing fast-pour beer outlets that serve *radlers* (half beer, half lemon-lime soda), *helles*, and *Russiches* beers by the Maß-ful. Take-out, fast food stands offer tasty and economical fare. Russiches, by the way, is a *weiß* or wheat beer, that is also mixed half-and-half with lemon-lime soda. Just as accessible are tall glass liter mugs of the more familiar Löwenbräu brew. The crowds are unusually large here, attracted by all that the beer garden has to offer coupled with its central location in Munich's largest public park. There's a carousel just for the kids. Also, it is the only Englischer Garten beer bazaar readily adjacent to public transportation (a bus stop just behind the beer garden). Chinesischer Turm is a marvelous place for people watching, where the beer is bountiful and the well-shaded setting could hardly stand improvement. It ranks a hefty 4-1/2 beer rating.

Chinesischer Turm
Englischer Garten 3
8000 Munich 22

(089) 395028

Lowenbrau

10 a.m. to 1 a.m.

7000 in Beer Garden

# Seehaus
## in Englischer Garten

*A* surprising number of visitors to Englischer Garten overlook what one local scribe has termed "the most beautiful interlude in Munich". Seehaus is certainly that, and to stop short of this marvelous, lush green lakeside gem is to forego a rare opportunity to savor mouth watering traditional Bavarian fare along with liters of a top variety local brew, Paulaner. It's all available in an idyllic setting of abundant shade-bearing chestnut trees that ring the beer garden, right up to the water's edge.

Alas, the nearby Chinesischer Turm is to blame. An ample experience in itself, the better-known Chinese Pagoda and beer garden often steal the limelight from Seehaus. Too many would-be seasoned beer drinkers fail to venture the several hundred yards farther to Seehaus. They should realize that, when it comes to the Englischer Garten, good things really do come in bunches. Four in this particular bunch, with Seehaus perhaps tops on the list. (Hirschau and Aumeister to come.)

The modernity of Seehaus' French-style cafe-restaurant belies the 200-year history behind this establishment. It began as a converted wood building left over from a nearby dairy farm in 1791. Pressed into service as an inn, the building housed the first beer-dispensing outlet in 1811 and served local patrons well for most of the next century. In 1882-83 the local architect Gabriel von Seidl built the nearby boathouse on Kleinhesseloher

**Seehaus beer garden on the banks of Kleinhesseloh See.**

Lake — in use today — and the restaurant was reconstructed in 1935. The existing facility is of recent vintage, built in 1985.

Today, Seehaus caters to a middle- to upper-class crowd, even offering the ultimate Yuppie treat, a frozen yogurt stand! Adjacent boat rentals allow one to work up an appetite along with a mammoth thirst, all easily satisfied by the sustenance Seehaus has to offer.

The restaurant is a bit pricey, in contrast to the self-service food stand that appeals to a more pedestrian pocketbook. Paulaner beer, a choice brew, is the beer of choice at this establishment. The increasingly popular, and still good tasting, "Paulaner Light" (with 40 percent less alcohol and calories) is an added plus for those who want to make the day last.

If one were limited to visit only one beer garden in Munich — a depressing thought — this would be at the very top of the list. When the weather is warm and the throat dry, there is no better alternative than Seehaus. It's the best of the Englischer Garten. Five beers and a helping of O'batzer on the side!

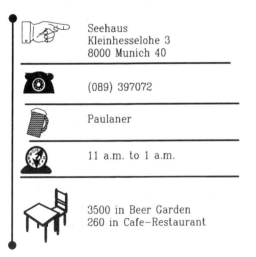

Seehaus
Kleinhesselohe 3
8000 Munich 40

(089) 397072

Paulaner

11 a.m. to 1 a.m.

3500 in Beer Garden
260 in Cafe-Restaurant

# Hirschau
## in Englischer Garten

*A* disco beer garden? Samstag Nacht fever and twirling lederhosen? Take a walk over the pedestrian bridge just behind Seehaus, follow the pathway to the right and find out. Hirschau, an otherwise traditional Munich beer garden, rocks Englischer Garten to a different beat most nights (Tuesday through Saturday) beginning at 8 p.m. when the band begins to play (3 p.m. on Sundays).

The indoor restaurant and beer stube offers dancing and listening enjoyment, spanning a wide range of musical tastes. The entertainment takes on a personal slant when the local proprietor takes up his own instrument to join in an impromptu musical jam session. The under 30 crowd is especially at home here, but there's plenty to attract the interest of families and other visitors to Hirschau. A children's play area on the premises, and a miniature golf course and tennis center next door round out a well-appointed beer garden.

Hirschau area was part of the old royal game preserves. The name is itself a derivative of the German term for deer blind or "Hirsch Au". The building housing the restaurant — reconstructed several times — was home to Munich's most avid sportsmen. One can imagine how they whiled away the evenings over a frothy mug or *Glühwein* (hot cinnamon-spiced red wine) commiserating over the one that got away. The hunt these days is more of the social variety and Hirschau has become an "in" meeting place. After 9 p.m. or so the clientele tilts heavily toward the young adult set.

The restaurant menu, in addition to a typical Bavarian selection, is spiced with an unusual variety of Yugoslavian dishes and an opportunity to sample east European cuisine, with lots of grilled meat entrees and zesty seasonings.

Hirschau tries to be all things to all people. With the diversity of its offerings, teamed with the Englischer Garten setting, it comes close. It rates a commendable 4 beers.

Hirschau
Gyslingstrasse 15
8000 Munich 40

(089) 369942

Spaten–Brau

11 a.m. to 1 a.m.
Closed on Mondays

1000 in Beer Garden
150 on the Terrace
280 in Restaurant

# *Aumeister*
## *in Englischer Garten*

*L* ast stop in the Englischer Garten, but never lagging in the hearts of Munich's beer garden fans, is Zum Aumeister. The old Munich tradition and atmosphere of a hospitable country inn is in evidence here today. The Aumeister dates back to 1810, when it was the region's primary hunting lodge and staging area for the duke's frequent hunts. As time went on, and the huntsmen began outnumbering the game, the lokal expanded its charter. The chase finally gave way to the dispensing of beer, and in 1914 the local hunting club was replaced with a full-time restaurant and beer garden. In 1959, the restaurant was completely rebuilt and a terrace garden was added.

The Aumeister, with its sizeable beer garden (2000 seats) and well-stocked self-service food stand (home-baked soft pretzels), deserves its reputation as one of the best-known and traditional beer gardens in all of Munich. The restaurant features seasonal dishes, including white *spargel* (asparagus), forest-grown mushrooms, and wild game.

The atmosphere is comfortable and serene, with adequate shade from mature chestnut trees and strategically located table umbrellas.

Unlike Englischer Garten's three other beer establishments, Aumeister draws patrons from a wider area of Munich and is a favored haunt of many northern city dwellers. It has the added advantage of easy accessibility by U-bahn (Studentenstadt), after a short walk through the garden.

This is a place for relaxation and convivial conversation. Although an institution among Munich's knowledgeable beer-drinking throngs, Aumeister is almost unknown to the city's foreign visitors. That is, until now. It draws a solid 4 beers and a high recommendation to be included in a full excursion to Munich's Englischer Garten.

Zum Aumeister
Sondermeierstrasse 1
8000 Munich 45

(089) 325224

Hofbrauhaus

9 a.m. to 11 p.m.

2000 in Beer Garden
(600 have table service)

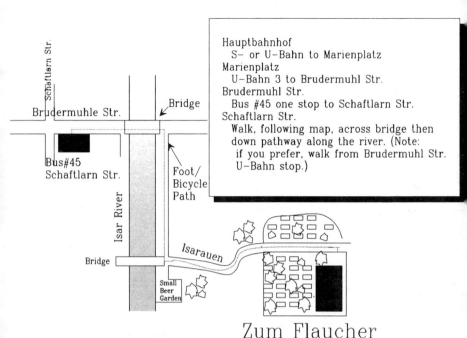

Hauptbahnhof
  S- or U-Bahn to Marienplatz
Marienplatz
  U-Bahn 3 to Brudermuhl Str.
Brudermuhl Str.
  Bus #45 one stop to Schaftlarn Str.
Schaftlarn Str.
  Walk, following map, across bridge then
  down pathway along the river. (Note:
  if you prefer, walk from Brudermuhl Str.
  U-Bahn stop.)

## Zum Flaucher

Zum Flaucher
Isarauen 1
8000 Munich 70

(089) 7232677

Lowenbrau

10 a.m. to 12 midnight

2000 in Beer Garden
85 in Restaurant

# Flaucher

*A* walk along the Isar canal, and then a left through the woods, leads to Zum Flaucher beer garden. One of Munich's oldest, Flaucher is a favorite haunt of bicyclists and hikers who spend the day among the greenery and the afternoon in the shade of a chestnut tree or an umbrella in the beer garden. It is a pocket of activity in an expanse of secluded park and woodland, with plenty of nearby recreational opportunities, including a meandering network of walking and biking trails.

Flaucher's beer garden covers a wide area, and rows of tables and benches spill over to the other side of the road. The restaurant is primarily a self-service, fast-food affair, but an outdoor full-service dining area is also available. The posted menu lists a hearty assortment of Bavarian beer snacks, and for seafood lovers roasted mackerel on a stick is a special treat. There is a play area for kids.

The beer garden and restaurant complex are in one of the city's more scenic woodland areas. The 10-minute walk from the nearest bus or U-bahn stop is a pleasant trek along the river canal and through the forest. Flaucher is a popular and well-known beer garden among Munich's citizenry. Yet it is seldom mentioned in the city's travel guides and is practically unknown to outsiders. It's hard to fathom, because this spacious, comfortable beer haven is definitely worth a visit.

The proprietor is interested in attracting more foreign visitors, although his current business is thriving. He ought to be taken up on the invitation. Flaucher, a shaded summertime sanctuary with good food, beer and relaxing atmosphere, gets 4 beers.

Zum Flaucher is one of Munich's most traditional beer gardens.

49

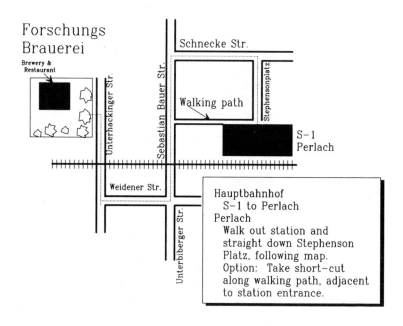

# Forschungs Brauerei

**Brewery & Restaurant**

Schnecke Str.

Unterhackinger Str.

Sebastian Bauer Str.

Stephensonplatz

Walking path

S-1
Perlach

Weidener Str.

Unterbiberger Str.

Hauptbahnhof
 S-1 to Perlach
Perlach
 Walk out station and
 straight down Stephenson
 Platz, following map.
 Option: Take short-cut
 along walking path, adjacent
 to station entrance.

Forschungsbrauerei
Unterhachinger Strasse 76
8000 Munich 83

(089) 6701169

St. Jacobus, brewed
on the premises

Tues.-Sat.: 11 a.m. to 11 p.m.
Sun./Hol.: 10 a.m. to 10 p.m.
Closed on Mondays

450 in Beer Garden
330 in Restaurant

# Forschungsbrauerei

*I*n the world of modern research, a small ante room belongs to the process of making beer. Forschungsbrauerei, strictly translated, "experimental brewery", has made a niche for itself, advancing the art along with the science. It's the little brewery that could, matching and surpassing Munich's industrial brewing giants in quality, but choosing to remain small and undiluted by the effects of mass production. So, while the big guys are up to their fill-lines with bottling and exporting demands, Forschungsbrauerei focuses its efforts on a small, select group of customers. Beer drinkers lucky enough to know of this suburban Munich establishment are rewarded with a home-brewed product manufactured and sold solely within the confines of the restaurant and beer garden.

Give credit to Gottfried Jakob whose profit motive was tempered by his credo that he'd never brew a bad glass of beer. In 1924 with diploma in the liberal libation arts in hand, the Weihenstephan-trained Gottfried began experimenting with a small 44-gallon beer making plant. He dispensed the fermented drink sparingly at first, to family and close friends. With each improved formula, Jakob built his own ladder to beer brewing success and demand for his brew grew faster than his laboratory could handle. In 1936 he began a commercial venture, a 500-gallon capacity brewery. At the same time he added a five-table restaurant.

That essentially marked the end of Jakob's grandiose plans for major expansion. He kept the business based on two personal principles: he would not compromise on the quality of his beer, and he would keep the entire operation within the capability of his family. Jakob never strayed from that path.

Gottfried Jakob passed on in 1958 and left the business to his son Heinrich who now runs the brewery with the help of brother-in-law Sigmund and one apprentice. Heinrich's wife Karin and sister Lieselotte operate the kitchen and office. Son Stefan mans the beer *ausschank*. The family is proud that they operate no retail outlet, no beer tents and no other guest houses. Their locally and rightfully famous *Pilsissimus* and *St. Jakobus* bock beers

51

are reserved for the fortunate few: those who are there to enjoy it.

The restaurant is basic and the menu is a mimeographed sheet highlighting daily specials that are cheap, filling, and tasty. The beer garden has room to seat thousands, but in character the proprietors have kept it to a manageable 500-600 or so. The two-story copper brewing plant at one end of the restaurant seems to gravity feed the entire beer garden, where beer is only served in the traditional and seldom seen clay-fired beer mugs. (Most Munich establishments have gone for the clear, 1-liter glass mugs that are more eye-appealing but less efficient in maintaining the freshness and cold temperature of the beer.)

For at least one week in the year, Forschungsbrauerei not only tries harder but succeeds over the big Munich breweries. The strong beer or "double-bock" season, a two-week period beginning around "Joseph's Day" on the 19th of March, is well celebrated by Münchners. Forschungsbrauerei's St. Jakobus bock beer (6% alcohol) is especially popular then. But while the rest of Munich is restricted to the 14-days of stark bier revelry, Forschungs is allowed an extra week of celebration. For an uncertain reason that is best explained as tradition, the brewery begins its party a week early, thus gaining the spotlight while the big houses downtown are still lining up entertainment and stringing decorations. Score one for the little guys.

Forschungsbrauerei is an unusual and rare find. The freshness of its product and the personal touch of the family-run business see to that. It's a moderate S-bahn ride and a short walk from the station in Perlach. Definitely worth an experimental visit to find out what the Jakob family will brew up next. Forschungsbrauerei gets a 4-beer rating.

Forschungsbrauerei, right, is famous for its St. Jakobus beer brewed on the premises. The small brewery in the Munich suburb of Perlach sponsors special festivities during the spring *Starkbierzeit*.

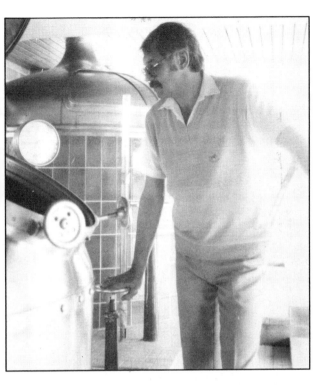

Sigmund Steinbeisser (left) inspects brewing paraphernalia at the family-run operation.

The beer garden (below), as seen from atop the *Südhaus* (main brewing plant) at Forschungsbrauerei

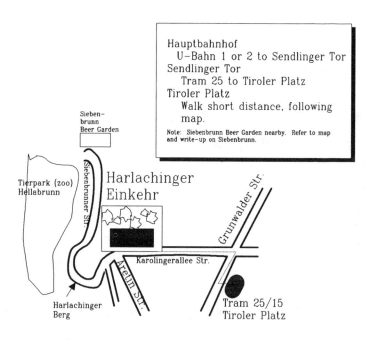

Hauptbahnhof
    U–Bahn 1 or 2 to Sendlinger Tor
Sendlinger Tor
    Tram 25 to Tiroler Platz
Tiroler Platz
    Walk short distance, following map.

Note: Siebenbrunn Beer Garden nearby. Refer to map and write–up on Siebenbrunn.

Harlachinger
Einkehr

Tierpark (zoo)
Hellabrunn

Sieben-
brunn
Beer Garden

Siebenbrunner Str.

Grunwalder Str.

Karolingerallee Str.

Areun Str.

Harlachinger
Berg

Tram 25/15
Tiroler Platz

Harlachinger Einkehr
Karolinger Allee 34
8000 Munich 90

(089) 646036

Lowenbrau

11 a.m. to 1 a.m.

1000 in Beer Garden
200 in Restaurant

# Harlichinger Einkehr

Harlichinger Einkehr is a beer garden that, like Siebenbrunn about a quarter-mile away, can be enjoyed as a logical stop-off during a visit to Hellabrunn zoo. Whereas Siebenbrunn is located at the entrance to the animal park, Harlichinger Einkehr is on a hill overlooking the entire complex. The establishment is a favorite starting or ending point for strollers and zoo visitors, with the added attractions of mini-golf, tennis and a horse-riding stable next door.

The restaurant and beer garden have been recently renovated, with much of the old charm of a traditional Bavarian outdoor eatery left intact. The outdoor grill station and fast-food stand offer the usual array of sumptuous fare, including mackerel on a stick and specially prepared roast duck.

Evidently the proprietors have concluded that the kids have been left to wander endlessly among the animal exhibits, because no children's play area is provided. The unusual number of round-table *stammtischs* in the beer garden attests to the popularity of Harlichinger Einkehr to an army of regular customers. League-sanctioned card games are always in vogue here and the bend in the road marks a comfortable corner lokal frequented by loyal neighborhood stalwarts.

Harlichinger Einkehr is a slice of everyday life in Munich. Few tourists venture here, but many more should. The *wirt* or owner is friendly and always interested in opening his doors to an international clientele. A visit would be augmented greatly if made in tandem with Siebenbrunn, just down the road. Public transportation is as near as the corner and the beer garden is a prime candidate for a fast dash for a cold beer and a decent meal at a very reasonable price. Harlichinger Einkehr rates 3 beers which makes it worthy of a visit but even more inviting if paired with Siebenbrunn nearby.

Hauptbahnhof
  U-Bahn 1 or 2 to
  Sendlinger Tor
Sendlinger Tor
  U-Bahn 6 to
  Munchener
  Freiheit
Munchener Freiheit
  Exit U-Bahn
  station on
  Leopold Strasse.
  Beer lokal is
  around the corner
  on Franz Str.

Leopold Str.

Franz Str.

U-Bahn 3 or 6
Munchener Freiheit

# Haus der
# 111 Biere

Haus der 111 Biere
Franz Str. 3
8000 Munich 40

(089) 331248

111 different brands

5 p.m. to 1 a.m.

250 at bars and tables
on two floors

# Haus der 111 Biere

$\mathcal{M}$ unich is a city of superlatives — the world's largest beer garden, biggest beer hall, and, yes, the greatest beer selection under one roof. The Haus der 111 Biere (no translation needed) is a paragon of truth in advertising. Conveniently located around the corner from a U-bahn stop (Münchner Freiheit), the lokal is appropriately smack in the middle of Schwabing's student quarter. The two-story establishment offers a beer list from A to Z — "Andechser Bergbock" (#81) to "Zauberer Bier" (#9) — and alphabetical selections in between, from 25 countries around the world. Eight beers on tap, and 103 more in bottles and cans, make this the ideal place for those who love beer, but just can't make up their minds which one they love the best.

Tiger beer from Singapore, Elephant beer from Denmark, Sapporo from Japan, Bohemia from Mexico, Tsingtao from China, Porteris from Russia, Harley Davidson Heavy and (now get this) Nude Beer from America . . . all just for starters. Is it any wonder that the place is overflowing with a clamorous crowd whose call for "just one more" is as much a challenge as it is a request.

Not to say that there aren't plenty of local brews poured here. Haus der 111 Biere sports a menu filled with the best brews Munich and all of Germany have to offer. The walls are covered with beer memorabilia with an international theme. The lokal itself has a comfortable English-pub decor, including teakwood bars (one on each floor) surrounded by private tables and booths where customers can scan the list for their next taste test. The clientele are a mix of local students and curious foreigners attracted by the chance to rekindle forgotten taste-buds with some back-home brew or christen new ones with libations from around the globe.

Selection has its price, and nothing on the menu comes for less than DM 5 or 6 (up to 12 to 14 for the more exotic brands). There is no beer garden here, but plenty of indoor room, making this an ideal location for a winter or rainy weather visit. Some micro-nuked snacks are available, but this is not a preferred elective for satisfying a hearty appetite.

Shortcomings exist in the paltry food selections, the accelerated pace of a rising bar tab and the relatively limited seating on a crowded weekend evening. It lacks the traditional ambience of other Munich beer establishments and, sure, someone will find a place with even more beers on the menu. Yet, Haus der 111 Biere is a great place to meet and mingle with a lively, predominantly younger crowd . Anything but boring, it stays several six-packs ahead of the nearest competition. It's an especially good alternative when variety and not economy is the goal. Decisions, decisions . . . it gets 3-1/2 beers.

# Gasthof Hinterbruhl

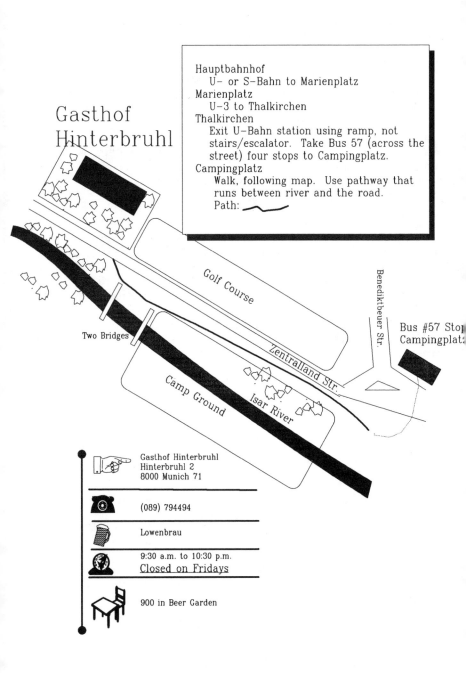

Hauptbahnhof
  U- or S-Bahn to Marienplatz
Marienplatz
  U-3 to Thalkirchen
Thalkirchen
  Exit U-Bahn station using ramp, not stairs/escalator. Take Bus 57 (across the street) four stops to Campingplatz.
Campingplatz
  Walk, following map. Use pathway that runs between river and the road.
  Path: ～

Golf Course

Benediktbeuer Str.

Bus #57 Stop
Campingplatz

Two Bridges

Zentralland Str.

Camp Ground

Isar River

Gasthof Hinterbruhl
Hinterbruhl 2
8000 Munich 71

(089) 794494

Lowenbrau

9:30 a.m. to 10:30 p.m.
Closed on Fridays

900 in Beer Garden

# Hinterbrühl

*T*ired of city life? Wish you could find a little alpine redoubt but no time for a trip to Garmisch, Berchtesgaden or some other Bavarian mountain resort? Hinterbrühl is a low-altitude, high-atmosphere facsimile of the above, and a whole lot easier to get to. It's hard to believe this "mountain lodge" on the banks of the Isar is actually within Munich's city limits (Thalkirchen district). It seems a world and several topographical elevations apart. The 160-year-old, three-story restaurant and beer tavern has more the look of a way-station where knapsackers stop to pitch a lean-to and *lederhosen* and spiked climbing boots are the preferred dress over shirt-sleeves and tennis

shoes. A backdrop of a pine-forested hillside adds to the effect as does a 900-seat beer garden overlooking the river. Those seated nearest the river's edge in summer are treated to a constant parade of party rafters (*Flöß*) where the conversation is punctuated every 10 minutes or so by the gradually rising crescendo of an approaching water-borne "oom-pah" band. For a fleeting moment, river-going rafters and landlubber *biergartlers* share a camaraderie in a raised glass of beer and several harmonious bars of a traditional German drinking song before the raft and its revelers disappear in the distance. That is, until the next raft, the next song, and the next beer.

Hinterbrühl's history is a common one: a down-river stopover along the main logging route between the upper forested areas and the lumber mills below. The lumberjack clientele has been replaced with a devoted following of city-slickers, and the process itself is embodied in the still flourishing custom of *Flöß*. Yet, the original forest atmosphere remains.

In a little-known historical footnote, Hinterbrühl was once a favorite haunt of Nazi officialdom before and during World War II. The likes of Hitler, Göring and Goebbels were frequent visitors as they considered this a suitable alternative when political business kept them away from their more opulent mountain chalets nestled among Berchtesgaden's picturesque snow-capped peaks. When the war ended and scores were settled, 10 Nazis went to the gallows in October 1946. Göring cheated the hangman's rope by committing suicide in his cell. His ashes, along with those of the other Nazi war criminals were strewn into the *Weuzbach*, a stream that runs alongside Hinterbrühl.

Hinterbrühl today is no shrine to anything but outdoor beer drinking enjoyment. The location of this restaurant and beer garden is ideal for long walks along the river, through the woods and general communing with nature. One of the city's largest camping areas, an 18-hole golf course, and the Tierpark Hellabrunn (zoo) are all nearby. The restaurant offers a limited menu but daily specials. The beer garden serves wood-grilled specialties, including roast pork knuckles, chicken and a variety of sausages. Strangely, the entire operation shuts down on Fridays, an important note to remember to avoid a weekend disappointment.

Hinterbrühl is high on tradition and atmosphere in a rare wooded setting that puts the Bavarian alpine region a short U-bahn and bus ride away. It's one of the best in Munich, earning a well-deserved 4-1/2 beers.

Patrons at Gasthof Hinterbrühl are afforded a tableside view of the unique Münchner tradition of *Floß*, or party rafting. At the height of the summer season, rafts fully laden with beer and beer drinkers float by every 10 minutes.

# Hirschgarten

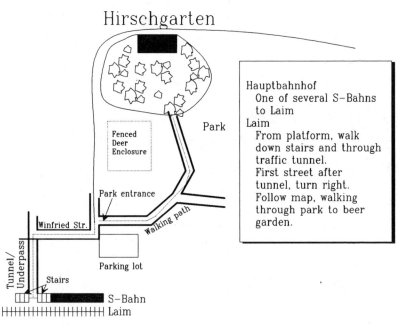

Park

**Hauptbahnhof**
One of several S-Bahns to Laim

**Laim**
From platform, walk down stairs and through traffic tunnel.
First street after tunnel, turn right.
Follow map, walking through park to beer garden.

Fenced Deer Enclosure

Park entrance

Winfried Str.

Tunnel/Underpass

Stairs

Parking lot

S-Bahn
Laim

Hirschgarten
Hirschgarten 1
8000 Munich 19

(089) 172591

Augustiner Edelstoff

10 a.m. to 11 p.m.

8000 in Beer Garden
320 in Restaurant

# Hirschgarten

$\mathcal{T}$ he Hirschgarten is the biggest beer garden in the world, and doesn't even bother to brag about it. The proprietors have decided the money they save on advertising and glitzy brochures is better spent financing an army of service help to manage the 8,000 guests who invade this place on warm weekend afternoons. This former royal hunting preserve packs them in, beer mug to beer mug, tighter than salt on a pretzel.

As big as it is, the beer garden and restaurant occupy a small parkland corner of the palatial grounds surrounding Schloß Nymphenburg. Nearby are lakes, gushing fountains, botanical gardens, parks and of course the palace itself.

Nymphenburg is one of the more opulent among the Wittlesbach stable of royal redoubts. It was built in 1664 as a present to the Electress Henriette Adelaide for having given birth to a long-awaited son, Max Emanuel, who would eventually ascend the throne. The palace became the favored summer retreat of several generations of Bavarian ruling families. Within the mirrored halls and gold-leaf and fleur-de-lis embellished ceilings is a unique set of paintings: King Ludwig I's "Gallery of Beauties". The paintings are Ludwig's choice of the most beautiful women in Munich. Those

**A round of cheer is a round of beer and a hearty *Prosit!* in the Hirschgarten.**

he personally selected to pose for portrait painter Joseph Stieler included his own daughter-in-law, ladies at court and Lola Montez, the royal mistress (see Menterschwaige).

With Ludwig's well-known love for Munich's beer gardens, it's no wonder that a section of this massive estate was dedicated to the outdoor beer-drinking art. The beer garden is so large to be split up in areas of shade, sun and a section of tables with an overhead, retractable ramada standing by in case of any sudden afternoon cloudbursts. Service is available at those covered tables nearest the restaurant. Most, however, are *selbstbedienung* (self-service) and patrons sitting there are welcome to bring their own picnic baskets and wait on themselves. They begin by selecting a glass, liter mug from the rack at the side of the row of fast-food stands. Tradition calls for washing the mug in the steel basins provided (more like rinsing in cold water) and walking around the corner to the *ausschank* for a fill-up of fresh, cold Augustiner beer right from the wooden keg.

The self-serve, cafeteria style row of snack stands offers a wide assortment of Bavarian foods. Lots of sausages, spit-roasted whole chickens, and meat and potato salads are on sale. There's also a mouth-puckering rich cream cheese called *Obatzer* worth trying. It goes great as a spread over torn-off sections of fresh-baked salted pretzel (*Bretz'n*). Fish lovers have only to follow their nose when the mackerel-on-a-stick stand is in operation. The aroma of roasting seafood permeates the entire beer garden.

The in-door restaurant at the far end of Hirschgarten has managed a gourmet reputation of its own. Unlike many of Munich's beer gardens, the restaurant here has won the support of a loyal clientele that keeps it open

**The deer that give Hirschgarten its name are real and a special attraction for the kids.**

and busy during the winter months when the rest of the beer garden is closed.

The Hirschgarten or "deer garden" actually lives up to its name. At the edge of the beer garden is an enclosure housing dozens of live, well-domesticated Bambis who like to stick their noses through the fence and munch on handouts from passersby. This informal petting zoo is a treat for the kids and a reminder of local history. Centuries ago the Hirschgarten was a staging area for the king's royal hunts. The local four-legged game have nothing to fear these days. They're well protected and cared for and kept off the restaurant's menu.

Hirschgarten is the type of beer garden that Munich is famous for: huge, inviting and filled with tradition. Local management isn't hurting for patronage, so they are less keen than most in attracting the notice of the city's hype-conscious tourist industry. One result is that few foreign visitors venture here. They just haven't known about Hirschgarten or how accessible it is with public transportation. (A 10-minute S-bahn ride and a short walk from the busy commuter stop at Laim — pronounced "Lime".)

It's no wonder bragging rights are conferred upon the patrons and not the proprietors of Hirschgarten. With a can't-miss combination of Munich's best-tasting beer, plenty of outstanding eats, and an atmosphere without room for much improvement, word-of-mouth testimonials are all that's needed. Hirschgarten gets the top 5-beer rating.

**Visitors to Hirschgarten are treated to the vanishing custom of a trip to the** *Kruge* **rack to select their own liter glass mug. A quick rinsing, and then around the corner to the beer** *ausschank* **for a fill-up.**

Hauptbahnhof
    Walk up Bayer Str. (see inset map)
    through Marienplatz and follow main map

                    OR
Hauptbahnhof
    Take one of several S- or U-Bahns direct
    to Marienplatz
Marienplatz
    Walk, following main map

# Hofbrauhaus

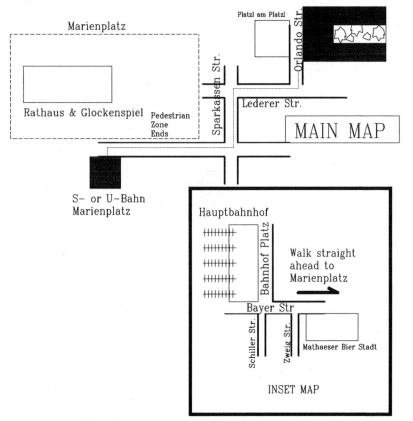

Marienplatz

Platzl am Platzl

Orlando Str.

Rathaus & Glockenspiel

Pedestrian
Zone
Ends

Sparkassen Str.

Lederer Str.

## MAIN MAP

S- or U-Bahn
Marienplatz

Hauptbahnhof

Bahnhof Platz

Walk straight
ahead to
Marienplatz

Bayer Str

Schiller Str.

Zweig Str.

Mathaeser Bier Stadt

INSET MAP

# Hofbräuhaus

**N**o beer establishment in Munich is more renowned, revered — and reviled — than the Hofbräuhaus. To some, the world-famous beer hall is an artificial plastic replica of a real Munich beer hall, wheeled out on an hourly basis for the amusement of a rotating fleet of bused-in tourists. A reasonable facsimile and not much more. To others it's a veritable shrine to the brewing and beer-drinking arts, worthy of more than a few genuflects from those faithful pilgrims fortunate enough to pass through its Gothic portals. But defenders and detractors take note. The truth, somewhere in the middle, is rendered moot by a Hofbräuhaus that is rafter to rafter, uncompromising and unrelenting fun!

On any given afternoon and evening, a world community, from Americans to Zambians (and more than a few touring Germans), gathers here to hoist a mug, join in a round of "Oans, Zwoa, Gsuffa" and become — if only for the moment — honorary, card-carrying Bavarians. And if the Hofbräuhaus isn't rollicking, pulsating fun the way Munich beer halls really are, then maybe it's the way they ought to be: a place where everybody is welcome and nobody goes away disappointed. The beer and food are plentiful and the high-charged atmosphere is the closest thing to a real party this side of Oktoberfest.

Despite the artificial veneer left from decades of commercialization, the history of this beer-drinking mecca is without question. Bavarian Duke Wilhelm V founded the *Hofbräu* or central brewing house in 1589. Two years later the brewery began producing limited libations for an elite royal clientele, but by 1604 was "exporting" its product beyond the city limits. Soon thereafter the first bock beer was brewed here and, since it was commonly dispensed beginning in May, earned the name *Maibock*. In 1610 the

Hofbrauhaus
Am Platzl
8000 Munich 2

(089) 221676

Hofbrauhaus

9 a.m. to 12 midnight

700 in Beer Garden
900, 1500 in Ballrooms

royal brewery expanded its business beyond the Bavarian aristocracy and embraced the thirsty common folk, thus founding its reputation as the "people's brew". When rampant mid-19th century inflation threatened to place beer among a growing list of unattainable luxuries, a royal decree was issued freezing the brew-house's prices and preserving for "the military and working classes a healthy and wholesome drink". A good thing, too, because lesser provocations were stirring revolution all over Europe. The Bavarians, with a Hofbräuhaus continuing to dispense their venerable brew at dependable prices, remained contented and left the militant unpleasantries to their Prussian cousins up north.

The Hofbräuhaus was moved to its present location in 1828 and rebuilt in much its current style in 1897. In the years just after World War I, this was the site for much plotting and intrigue. Hitler and his fledgling Nazi party moved their political rallies to the Hofbräuhaus' spacious inner sanctum when his fiery oratory began drawing large crowds. The blood-red, white and black banners with the Nazi *Hackenkreuz* (Swastika) were an oft-seen adornment to the eaves of the Hofbräuhaus during the years between the wars. As if paying the price for the conflagration that followed, the Hofbräuhaus was 60 percent destroyed in World War II and not completely rebuilt until the late-1950s.

Today it is a meeting place for the world. Visitors to its cavernous beer hall, restaurant, beer garden, and second-story massive festival hall will sense the history behind this place — despite the touristy surface outer layer. But along with a perception of the past is a wonderful enjoyment of

**A Sunday afternoon at Munich's Hofbräuhaus around the turn of the century.**

the present.    Like no other place on earth, fun is infectious at the Hofbräuhaus.    At some time during the evening, you will fall prey and become one of the crowd of singing, shouting, swaying beer drinkers.  Since chances of being left a table to one's self are slim, the opportunity for striking up conversations with fellow travelers in a multitude of languages is practically assured.  (Here you would even be forgiven for sitting, unknowingly of course, at a *Stammtisch* for *der Altbayern*, a table reserved for genuine Bavarian aboriginals.)  If you don't think you'll get caught up in all of it, you just haven't been there yet.

One young visitor from Sweden did.  He made beer-drinking history at the Hofbräuhaus when he set the world record for fastest chug-a-lug of a one-liter stein of beer.  The 22-year-old med student accomplished the feat in 4.4 seconds.  (Kids, don't try this one at home!)

The Hofbräuhaus lives up to all its billing as a "must-see' on every travel itinerary computer print-out.  Passing this off as a commercialized tourist trap would be missing the point:  Hofbräuhaus is a cauldron of bubbling fun and enjoyment, spiced with good beer, food and all that one could ever ask of a Munich beer hall.  You'll never have a bad time here.  It's tops, 5 beers without question.

A 1929 postcard depicts HB's massive festival hall in an earlier era.

69

Hauptbahnhof
  U-Bahn 4 or 1 to Max-Weber Platz
Max-Weber Platz
  Walk out exit to Innere Wiener Str.,
  Follow map below

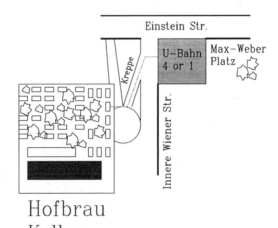

Einstein Str.

Kreppe

U-Bahn 4 or 1

Max-Weber Platz

Innere Wiener Str.

# Hofbrau Keller

Hofbraukeller
Am Wiener Platz
Haidhausen
8000 Munich 80

(089) 4487376

Hofbrauhaus

8:30 a.m. to 12 midnight

1900 in Beer Garden
780 in Restaurant

# Hofbräu Keller

$\mathcal{A}$ sk any tourist to name a famous beer lokal in Munich and the answer is predictable: Hofbräuhaus. Ask a Münchner the same question and you might get a surprise. The initiated and well-saturated among the local populace might just as likely list the Hofbräu Keller. This sprawling restaurant and beer garden on Max Weber Platz is still frequented by a large number of urban dwellers who want a taste of traditional *Gemütlichkeit* without having to travel long distances to enjoy it.

Predictably, the "keller" versus the "haus" leans heavily on the outdoor beer garden atmosphere to attract its clientele. Not without its roots in local history, HB keller is just around the corner from the site of the infamous Burgerbräu Keller, where in 1923 Hitler hatched his thwarted "Beer Hall Putsch." While the Burgerbräu has been leveled and a modern cultural center erected in its place, the Hofbräu Keller has survived. But just barely. Built in 1893, the beer emporium flourished for many years and became a well-frequented haven for Munich's cultural elite. As the center of activity shifted to other sections of the city, the Hofbräu Keller fell on hard times. The imposing multi-story building that houses the restaurant and banquet hall was totally bombed out during World War II. Just when it looked safe to go back into the beer garden, another stroke of bad luck occurred in 1987 when a fire gutted a portion of the main structure to the bare stone of its foundation.

Still, it came back. Its present proprietors, Ulrike and Georg Sandbichler, are proud that their historic beer garden is back in full operation. Considering the devastation, Hofbräu Keller retains much of the old charm, and the interior rooms appear unscathed from the time when the intelligentsia and political movers and shakers from all over Munich were counted among its devoted followers.

The refurbishment goes on, and the constant reconstruction is a distraction to the casual visitor. The outside paint is peeling and the self-service food stands are insufficient. Also without benefit is the enclosed setting: the beer garden, while well-shaded and spacious, suffers from encroaching buildings and a neighborhood in obvious decline.

Nevertheless, tenacity breeds admiration and this is an enduring facility, to be sure. It's easy to forgive the short-comings and make the most of a brief visit to so historic an establishment. The food served up in the restaurant and in the garden is excellent, and the beer, after all, is HB. Despite the hardship a trip to the Hofbräu Keller is worth the patronage, if only for the purpose of watching this poor cousin of its more-famous relative come back to life. All things considered the Hofbräu Keller rates an "A" for effort and 2-1/2 beers.

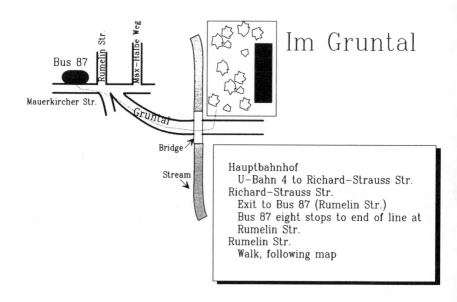

# Im Gruntal

Bus 87
Rumelin Str.
Max-Halbe Weg
Mauerkircher Str.
Gruntal
Bridge
Stream

Hauptbahnhof
  U-Bahn 4 to Richard-Strauss Str.
Richard-Strauss Str.
  Exit to Bus 87 (Rumelin Str.)
  Bus 87 eight stops to end of line at
  Rumelin Str.
Rumelin Str.
  Walk, following map

Im Gruntal
Im Gruntal 15
8000 Munich 81

(089) 980984

Paulaner

11 a.m. to 10 p.m.

1300 in Beer Garden
240 in Restaurant

# Im Grüntal

*I* m Grüntal owns the dubious distinction as the most expensive beer garden in Munich. At this writing a liter Maß of beer is DM 8, a hefty price, even by Munich standards. That may be just enough claim to fame to attract the *Biergarten-Schickeria* (beer garden chic) crowd, but there are other positive traits that appeal to the less-heeled among us. For one thing, the setting is right out of a Thoreau novel, complete with babbling brook running through the premises. In addition to some of the best Bavarian fare available anywhere, the restaurant sports a menu filled with international favorites, including French and Italian selections. The atmosphere is quiet, relaxing and seldom over-crowded. There is no self-service and picnic baskets are prohibited. However, the house makes up for this by providing excellent service and superior food that even *Oma* would have had trouble coming up with.

Im Grüntal's accommodating beer garden (1300 seats) is smartly landscaped and well-buffered from the residential area nearby. Here is a place where the focus is on relaxation and casual conversations. It's a great place to take a date you want to impress and a chance to hob-nob with Munich's upper-crust. Chances are the most prominent of the *prominente* will also appear the most casual. Although Im Grüntal stands several rungs up the price ladder, the atmosphere is laid-back and short-sleeve shirts with open collars are more than acceptable.

The restaurant and beer garden go back about 100 years which makes Im Grüntal a relative newcomer on the epicurean block. This is a place where gourmet tastes are satisfied and the beer (Paulaner) is one of the best in Munich. If only it weren't so damned expensive! Im Grüntal earns a less than frugal 3-1/2 beers.

# Getting to Kloster Andechs

From Munich Hauptbahnhof, take S-Bahn 5 to Herrsching (40 minutes).

Herrsching train station has taxi and bus service to Kloster Andechs. Metered taxi ride costs about DM 15 each way. City-run bus 951 runs several times a day, check schedule. However, more frequent service is provided by the private Rauner bus line. Look for the "H" bus stop that says "Rauner". Following is the Rauner line schedule:

### Rauner bus departs from Herrsching train station:

| | |
|---|---|
| **11:15 (Mon-Sat)** | **3:55 (Mon-Sat)** |
| 11:55 (Mon-Fri) | 5:15 (Sat only) |
| **1:15 (Mon-Sat)** | 5:33 (Mon-Fri) |
| **1:55 (Mon-Sat)** | **6:33 (Mon-Sat)** |

### Rauner bus returns from Kloster Andechs:

| | |
|---|---|
| 11:00 (Mon only) | **4:15 (Mon-Sat)** |
| 12:35 (Mon-Fri) | 5:30 (Sat only) |
| 1:30 (Mon-Sat, but not Tues & Fri) | 5:50 (Mon-Fri) |
| **1:54 (Mon-Sat)** | **6:45 (Mon-Sat)** |
| 2:10 (Sat only) | |

### Sundays and Holidays:

Depart Herrsching - 9:55, 11:15, 11:55, 1:15, 1:55, 2:35, 3:55, 4:35, 5:15, 6:33

Return from Andechs - 10:10, 11:40, 12:05, 1:30, 2:10, 2:55, 4:15, 4:55, 5:30, 6:45

Note: One-way ticket is approx. DM 2.

# Kloster Andechs

*K*loster Andechs was one of those best-kept secrets guarded — religiously no doubt — by the Benedictine brethren for centuries. On a hill overlooking the banks of the Ammersee, who could blame these monks 500 years ago for brewing the finest beer around, and then keeping it all to themselves. Then, in one of those historical acts of universal justice, Count Bertold IV decreed in 1128 that the monastic monopoly should end. His fiat required the most pious among his various fifedoms to make an annual pilgrimage, with cross and candle, to Andechs, a journey they welcomed with hardly a complaint.

Then, when a local legend began circulating that a blind woman from Widdersberg made the trek to Andechs and miraculously recovered her sight in 1274, business really took off. The brothers were suddenly swamped. In addition to holy relics, the religious visitors also began venerating the spirited brew.

Today, the "Sacred Mountain" plays host to thousands of modern day pilgrims, some there just to pray and meditate. The vast majority with more secular tastes comes to sample the local libation. Not that man lives by beer alone. The Kloster Andechs' 15th century Gothic church would make the pages of even the most discriminating tour book. The Benedictine abbey, endowed in 1455 as one of the last such monasteries of the Middle Ages, should not be overlooked. But, readers of this book are reminded to also consider the 3500-seat terraced beer garden that literally rings the church and monastic grounds.

Kloster Andechs
8131 Andechs

(08152) 1246

Andechser Special,
brewed on premises

9 a.m. to 8 p.m.

3500 in Beer Garden

The brewing tradition begun by monks in the 15th century was a natural offshoot of local farming activities. Beer was brewed on the premises as recently as 1972 when increasing demand caused the brothers to move the plant to a more spacious site—a meadow at the foot of the mountain—where they continue production today. Each year the brewery turns out 1.9 million gallons of beer, in five different varieties. Most of it is served in the monastery's centuries old *Bräustüberl* (beer hall) or in the brick-floored terrace beer garden. As one might expect, all is self-service here, including the food stands that offer a sturdy variety of Bavarian snacks. The beer is a little more potent than average and half-liter steins are available at all times. The real pleasure is to be able to sit back, relax and enjoy a tall cool one in a medieval setting with a commanding view of the entire valley. On a good day, the 270-degree panorama takes in the entire countryside, from Wendelstein to the Allgauer Alps.

The cloister has a gift and souvenir shop that sells mementos and books covering local history of the monastery and beer garden.

Kloster Andechs is a full-day journey, including a 40-minute train ride (S-Bahn 5) from the Hauptbahnhof to Herrsching. There is difficulty in finding a frequent bus that runs from Herrsching the several up-hill miles to the Kloster. Taxis are an alternative, but they run DM 15 each way. The city-run bus (951) is sporadic, to say the least, covering the route only two or three times a day. A more frequent and dependable choice is a private bus line (Rauner) that has a regular schedule directly to the Kloster Andechs. A ticket costs less than DM 2. For certain runs on certain days the MVV Tageskarte is honored as well (check with the driver when you board the bus). Thus, no map is required. However, the adjacent bus schedule will come in handy.

Kloster Andechs is truly a beer drinker's pilgrimage and well worth the extra effort and time to get there. The home-made beer is hearty and well-chilled, the atmosphere without equal. Religious beer-drinking experiences are hard to find. Andechs gets 4-1/2 beers.

"The Sacred Mountain" from a mid-17th century engraving .

Kloster Andechs, from an 1880 painting.

Kloster Andechs today: the scene of a little modern 'beer jousting'.

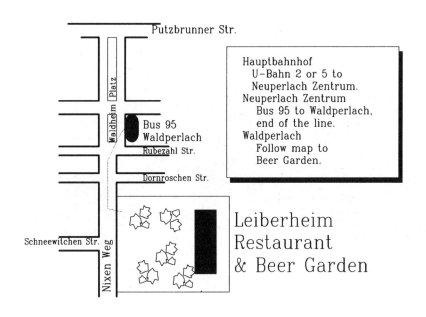

Putzbrunner Str.

Waldheim Platz

Bus 95
Waldperlach

Rubezahl Str.

Dornroschen Str.

Schneewitchen Str.

Nixen Weg

Hauptbahnhof
   U-Bahn 2 or 5 to
   Neuperlach Zentrum.
Neuperlach Zentrum
   Bus 95 to Waldperlach,
   end of the line.
Waldperlach
   Follow map to
   Beer Garden.

Leiberheim
Restaurant
& Beer Garden

Leiberheim
Nixenweg 9
8000 Munich 83

(089) 603295

Erhartinger Brau

11 a.m. to 11 p.m.

3000 in Beer Garden
60 in Restaurant

# Leiberheim

*W*hen Eduard Ordnung returned from World War I, without the use of his right leg and with an Iron Cross around his neck, a world-wide depression was looming. Even war heroes had to struggle to eke out a living in 1918 and Ordnung opened a beer garden in one of Munich's outlying suburbs. Leiberheim, named in honor of his wartime infantry unit, the Royal Bavarian Leibregiment, weathered the hard times and prospered. It is today one of Munich's largest beer gardens, and many would argue one of its most beautiful.

Among mixed stands of pine and chestnut trees, Leiberheim accommodates 3,000-plus visitors on summer afternoons. A restaurant that is 80 percent kitchen works overtime to service an outdoor terraced eating area as well as interior wood framed dinner nooks. The menu selection is small but hearty. The proprietor serves Bavarian-style dishes without making concessions to any volume-driven restaurant business. Outdoor food stands do the rest, and most of Leiberheim is on a self-service basis. The beer served is Erharting, from one of the area's smaller breweries.

The interior of the lokal is consumed mostly by a stage and auditorium used to host special Bavarian folklore programs. *Bayerischer Abends*, as they are known, are a speciality of Leiberheim during the winter months. The programs, usually lasting until late in the evening, feature semi-professional Bavarian entertainers in renditions of music, folk dancing and humorous skits (unless you're familiar with the language, most of the humor flies several feet above your head). The traditional folk theater was introduced at Leiberheim in 1920, with 215 "premiers" since 1946. Information and reservations can be had by calling 606-749.

Despite Leiberheim's upbeat atmosphere and lighthearted theatrical presentations, there are subtle and somber undertones. Inside the lokal, faded photographs and discolored paintings of military men grace the walls. In

**The endless card game is a daily ritual at Leiberheim.**

one corner, a glass-and-wood paneled display case houses full-dress military uniforms, dating back to before World War I. One, a captain's parade uniform with sword, dates back to 1912 and the last days of the Kaiser's Imperial Guard. Ordnung's Knight's Cross is on display, with other military artifacts. Ironically and tragically, Leiberheim's founder, who was wounded severely in 1916 during combat that earned him his high military honor, died in his sleep during a 1945 bombing raid at the close of World War II. It is in his spirit that a few of the old *Kameraden* still find their way to Leiberheim. These are men who grew up together, fought together, and now grow old together. They can be seen today, in the middle of a raucous card game, suddenly pausing to raise their glass and their voices to an old marching song in the memory of others who served and are now gone.

Ordnung's legacy lives on at Leiberheim, but not to the beat of a militant drum. The emphasis here is peaceful co-existence amid a patter of suburban socialization. Interestingly, the spacious beer enclave is able to thrive and prosper on a word-of-mouth existence. Available local tour guides seem bent on protecting its anonymity by ignoring one of the city's largest beer gardens. On the other hand, on those summer afternoons when 3,000 seats are barely enough, greater notoriety hardly seems a problem. When the roll call is sounded, Leiberheim stands at attention with 4 stalwart beers.

**Beer gardens like Leiberheim have a rich local tradition reaching back hundreds of years. This 1885 artist's rendering of an outdoor *Bayerischer Abend* illustrates the point.**

The founder's pre-World War I uniform is on display in the restaurant.

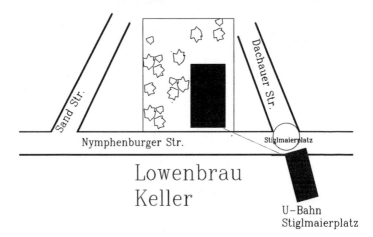

Hauptbahnhof
U–Bahn 1 to Stiglmaier Platz
Exit U–Bahn station on
Sitglmaier Platz.

Sand Str.

Dachauer Str.

Nymphenburger Str.

Stiglmaierplatz

Lowenbrau
Keller

U–Bahn
Stiglmaierplatz

Lowenbraukeller
Nymphenburger Strasse 2
8000 Munich 2

(089) 526021

Lowenbrau

9 a.m. to 1 a.m.

1800 in Beer Garden
2500 in Ballroom
500 in Banquet Rooms

# Löwenbräu Keller

*I* nternational name recognition. That's what Löwenbräu the
beer has. Few English-speaking visitors to Munich will fail to
recognize the famous "Lion's Brew" logo. And if they ask for it, few German-
speaking natives will likely understand them. What is commonly pronounced in English as "Low-in-brow" flows easily off the German tongue as
"Ler-vin-broy". Despite the dueling diphthongs, Löwenbräu ranks as
Germany's most notable liquid export (overseas licensing included). But
around home in Munich it is just another good-tasting beer, and by no
means the popular favorite. (Augustiner Edelstof holds that honor.)

Löwenbräu the beer hall and beer garden does much better. An annex
to the massive brewery on Nymphenburger Strasse, Löwenbräu Keller has
been a locally preferred beer oasis since it opened its doors for business on
June 14, 1883 with four regimental bands to mark the occasion. The original
structure was massive, with interior and beer-garden seating for some 8,000
guests, or about twice what is available today. On Dec. 17, 1944 a heavy
bombing raid reduced the huge *Festsaal* (ballroom) to rock and rubble.
Rebuilt after the war to smaller dimensions (encroachment from the thriving
brewery helped here), Löwenbräu Keller was reinstated with much of its

The Löwenbräu Keller from an old artist's rendering in 1885. The original facility
accommodated some 8,000 guests until it was heavily damaged in World War II.

83

original flavor and atmosphere. In 1986, a fire again destroyed part of the building, requiring yet more rebuilding and renovation. By 1987, the establishment was back together again, featuring a massive ballroom (2,000 seats) and a beer garden to accommodate 1,800 guests.

Löwenbräu Keller ranks as one of Munich's largest and most sumptuous. Its abundance of interior rooms (Stüben), cavernous restaurant and voluminous menu make this one of the city's most popular dining spots. The Pils-Pub, with its large circular bar, is a favorite with guests who want to quaff suds into the late evening. Returning home after one Maß too many is no problem since the nearest U-bahn stop is right across the street.

Löwenbräu Keller is filled with rooms and don't be shocked by the name of one of them. The Dachauer Stübe reflects a common German innkeeper's custom of adopting the names of surrounding villages. It is in no way itended to hallow the dark and historically brief period when the medieval town played unwilling host to the Third Reich's first and most-infamous concentration camp.

The beer garden is large though somewhat gerrymandered to fit within the confines of the available space and the large traffic artery that borders the entire brewery complex. On summer afternoons it is filled to capacity

The lion, a popular emblematic figure throughout southern Germany, is seen on the royal Bavarian coat of arms, along with the characteristic blue-and-white checkered pattern (eagles are favored up north). The king of beasts quaffing a mug of beer is the symbol of the Oktoberfest. (No, there never were lions roaming wild in pre-historic Germany.) The lion is a world-wide symbol of strength and potency, and a natural selection for ambitious princes and brewers alike.

with brewery and other blue-collar workers pausing for a refreshing break before heading home.

Two seasonal occasions are especially well celebrated at Löwenbräu Keller. When the Fasching or Carnival season (marking the beginning of Lent) reaches its peak in mid-February or early March, Löwenbräu Keller throws some of the rowdiest parties and masquerade balls in all of Munich. Several weeks later, in mid-March, the strong beer season (*Starkbierzeit*) begins and Löwenbräu Keller is again the scene of a little festive craziness.

Strong beer calls for strong men, and Steyrer Hans was by far mightiest of them all. Legend or history, probably a little of both, holds that one day in Löwenbräu Keller the Munich master butcher and lionized folk hero caused more than a few patrons to spill their beer by a feat of strength not equaled since. Hans, it is claimed — here comes the legend — was able to lift a 508-pound boulder with his middle finger! That late-19th century herculean feat has inspired the annual *Steinheberwettbewerb* at Löwenbräu Keller. The boulder lifting contest is a main attraction when the strong beer starts to flow. Contestants are given a break Hans never needed, because they are allowed to use both hands. Any lift of a foot or more is considered world-class and calls for the hoisting of several more liters of suds in celebration.

Löwenbräu Keller is a year-round attraction and the home of excellent traditional Bavarian cuisine along with the city's most widely dispensed beer. The lion on the label stands for a roaring good time. Löwenbräu Keller checks in with a 4-beer rating.

**Brewery Tours:** Löwenbräu offers tours year-round, except during Oktoberfest. The tours run regularly, beginning at 9:30 a.m. For a reservation or more information call 520-0496. Naturally, a chance to sample the product is included.

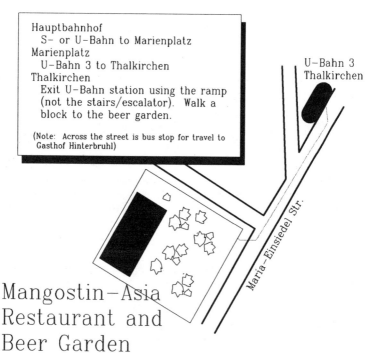

Hauptbahnhof
 S- or U-Bahn to Marienplatz
Marienplatz
 U-Bahn 3 to Thalkirchen
Thalkirchen
 Exit U-Bahn station using the ramp
 (not the stairs/escalator). Walk a
 block to the beer garden.

(Note: Across the street is bus stop for travel to
 Gasthof Hinterbruhl)

U-Bahn 3
Thalkirchen

Maria-Einsiedel Str.

# Mangostin-Asia
# Restaurant and
# Beer Garden

Mangostin-Asia
Maria-Einsiedel Strasse 2
8000 Munich-Thalkirchen

(089) 7232031

Lowenbrau

12 noon to 1 a.m.

550 in Beer Garden
220 in Restaurants

# Mangostin-Asia

*A* beer garden with ice carvings and sushi? Sounds like bar talk. And it was. Two home-grown Bavarians — one an accomplished chef, the other a savvy entrepreneur — wound up one evening at the same Bangkok bar several years ago. The conversation turned to what they both knew best — building a business and exotic Far Eastern cuisine. Why not an Asian beer garden in Munich no less?

Talk led to action and the result was "Thai Week" at Seehaus in Englischer Garten. The experimental oriental food fair was such a hit that the two budding businessmen pooled resources and began looking for other opportunities. The plan was to somehow take the traditional German beer garden and season it with the spice and flair of the Far East.

With the goal defined, Dr. Erich Kaub and Joseph Pete found a failing beer garden, bought it, and began renovating it. The two entrepreneurs developed rock gardens, water falls and fish ponds. They planted tropical ferns alongside domestic bushes, bamboo next to chestnut trees. The old restaurant was completely gutted and a new one molded in its place. Each renovated room was given a new Asian decor — gold-leaf dragons and red and black-varnished furnishings.

When Mangostin-Asia opened its doors in early spring 1990, Munich had never seen anything quite like it. The shaded traditional Bavarian beer garden had been absorbed completely into an oriental theme park where culinary tastes from east meet west.

The outdoor self-service food and drink stands of the Mangostin Garden offer an unusual choice of Mai-Tais from the tropical fruit bar or a fresh Maß of Löwenbräu beer. Inside are three more restaurants featuring original cuisine from Thailand, Japan, Malaysia, China, Indonesia and the Philippines. One, the Lemon Grass, offers Thai specialties, seafood, and "open Wok" Chinese cooking. Keiko Japanese restaurant dishes up sushi (raw fish), Tempura, and

**Whether Bavarian or Chinese, the lion guards the beer garden entrance.**

Sukiyaki. Papa Joe's Colonial Bar and Restaurant features snacks and hors d'oeuvres and plenty of comfortable rattan chairs for sitting around and enjoying exotic fruit-based cocktails (careful you don't poke your eye with an umbrella). The ice carvings, billed as the only such epicurean embellishments in all of Europe, begin as 5-ft.-high blocks of ice. The figures are chosen by customer request, carved and given a rotating place of honor in one of the restaurants.

Although Mangostin-Asia is new on the Munich scene, it is already earning a reputation the competition can only marvel at. In fact, there is no real comparison to this unique establishment. Word travels fast and during the summer months both the restaurant and beer garden fill up with the speed of a fast hand with an abacus board. Seats in the beer garden can be had on a first-come basis, but a table in one of the restaurants usually requires a reservation, or a long wait at the Colonial Bar. Inside prices are generally high, outside much more reasonable. No surprise for an establishment of this quality.

Mangostin-Asia is the best of not just both, but several worlds. It works on many different levels, one being that which appeals to lovers of Munich's beer gardens and lokals. The planners and builders of Mangostin-Asia were smart enough to augment but not replace the Bavarian beer garden experience. They have created that rare and truly distinctive atmosphere that has to be enjoyed to be appreciated. Mangostin-Asia gets an inscrutable 4-1/2 beer rating.

**Umbrellas in Mangostin's terrace dining area resemble those found in the drinks.**

A crowded beer garden on a warm afternoon is the ultimate experience for the "Ultimate Münchner".

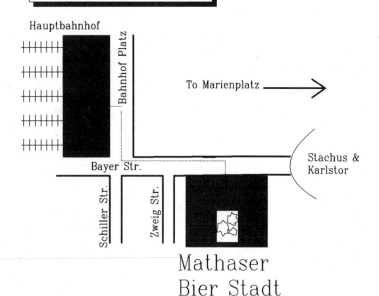

Hauptbahnhof
Walk, following map below

Hauptbahnhof

Bahnhof Platz

To Marienplatz →

Stachus &
Karlstor

Bayer Str.

Schiller Str.

Zweig Str.

## Mathaser Bier Stadt

Mathaser Bier Stadt
Bayer Strasse 5
8000 Munich 2

(089) 592896

Lowenbrau

10:30 a.m. to 12 midnight

250 in Beer Garden
5,000 in Beer Hall
1,400 in Ballroom

# Mathäser Bierstadt

*T*he odds-on favorite to rival the Hofbräuhaus for the affections of the world's beer-drinking public is Mathäser Bierstadt. In the past decade, Mathäser has come into its own as the alternate choice for a one-night this-is-all-of-Munich-you'll-ever-need-to-see attraction. And why not? This massive beer hall has plenty of potential: it's huge — seats 5,000, and rightly lives up to its claim as the "world's largest beer hall". It has music — a traditional Bavarian-style "oompah" band plays nightly in the beer hall. It has great food — at least two restaurants, a chance to order from a dictionary-length menu almost anywhere in the place, and one of the best streetside take-out, fast-food counters in Munich. So what's missing? In a word, service. The growling, rude, arrogant and aggressive waiters and waitresses at Mathäser detract considerably from what might otherwise be the most enjoyable and raucous in-door beer-drinking experience in all of Munich.

Despite the rude and at best apathetic treatment of its customers, Mathäser still manages to pack them in by the busloads. The place is usually filled to the rafters with tourists, out-of-town Germans and far too many local drunks. The nightly scene at Mathäser is high-pitched and rowdy, rivaling the Hofbräuhaus, but with all the crude, rough edges left intact. Fights are not uncommon and the hired help often act to separate the customers from each other and from tearing up the place. That does nothing to help their dispositions.

Still, the casual visitor with only a few hours to spend here will likely be impressed by the scope and breadth of Mathäser, the "beer city". The recommended approach would be to experience the pandemonium of the main beer hall, but to cushion it all with the refuge offered by the inner courtyard beer garden and the mezzanine restaurant. Also, the next door Weißbierkeller is a quiet cellar restaurant with excellent food and where, in fairness, the service is much better.

The festival hall (ballroom) is one of the largest in Munich (Zweigstraße entrance, backside of the beer hall). It offers weekend musical programs featuring big-name German bands that span the spectrum from swing, to rock, to country and western (yes, Germany has fallen in love with this patently American musical art form).

It's interesting that, where the Hofbräuhaus often takes its lumps for superficiality and commercialization, Mathäser could use a lot more of it. It existed in almost pure obscurity before World War II and like most of Munich was practically destroyed from wartime bombing raids. After spending some 12 million deutsche marks to rebuild the facility during the 1950's,

Mathäser's owners — an anonymous group — seemed to have left it on its own. Business flourished, customers grew, profits skyrocketed, and the service deteriorated. Maybe business has been too good. Unlike the most famous beer hall in the world, the largest beer hall in the world has somewhere lost the motivation and incentive to treat its customers — foreign and domestic — in a manner they are not only accustomed to, but also deserve. And that is truly a shame.

If enlightened management ever takes over Mathäser and spends some of those healthy profits on a few Dale Carnegie courses for its employees, then this monolithic beer establishment may just end up the best in Munich. Until then, it will have to get by on size alone. Turn a blind eye to the irascible service crew and look forward to a wild and rowdy night of fun and excitement at Mathäser Bierstadt. There are still plenty of redeeming qualities that earn it 3-1/2 slightly spilled beers.

**Mathaser "Beer City" was first a beer village, founded in 1829.**

Patrons gain their "15-minutes of fame" by ascending the bandstand and wielding the conductor's baton.

Mathäser's main hall (below) rings from the rafters with several thousand customers after a local soccer match. Mathäser earns its claim as "largest beer hall in the world".

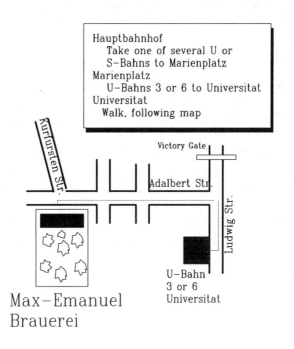

Hauptbahnhof
    Take one of several U or
    S-Bahns to Marienplatz
Marienplatz
    U-Bahns 3 or 6 to Universitat
Universitat
    Walk, following map

Kurfursten Str.

Victory Gate

Adalbert Str.

Ludwig Str.

U-Bahn
3 or 6
Universitat

## Max-Emanuel Brauerei

Max-Emanuel Brauerei
Adalbertstrasse 33
8000 Munich 40

(089) 2715158

Lowenbrau

10 a.m. to 10:30 p.m.

650 in Beer Garden
150 in Restaurant

94

# Max-Emanuel Brauerei

*M*ax-Emanuel Brauerei is a multi-faceted beer garden and student lokal in the heart of Schwabing, just down the street from Ludwig Straße and the Victory Arch. It's a student hang-out first class, but with a lot of extra appeal to a cross-section of Munich's beer garden crowd. For one thing, there's the beer garden itself, totally unexpected in this purely residential block of apartments. The well-shaded courtyard beer enclave serves up a choice of half or full liters of Löwenbräu beer and a rotating number of "blueplate" specials, including fish and vegetarian dishes. The outdoor restaurant adds a little zing to the standard Bavarian menu with Greek gyros dishes (mutton grilled on a revolving spit) with lots of tzatziki (a sauce made of yogurt and diced cucumber).

Indoors is a wood-paneled typical student lokal. There are sturdy oak tables and benches with carved initials or capsule messages from student Kilroys of bygone eras. During the afternoon and early evenings the lokal is dominated by the university crowd and affords an excellent opportunity for younger visitors to meet and get to know their Munich peer group. The conversations are friendly and many a university co-ed or local bohemian

**Max-Emanuel Brauerei: in the middle of Munich's student quarter.**

will welcome the chance to ply an English major or satisfy a lively curiosity regarding foreign guests.

In the evenings, the mood swings to dancing. Rock and roll and a "50s Record Hop" on Sundays, chic dance style of the month on Mondays, Wednesdays and Saturdays (would you believe Salsa?) and whatever else might be in temporary vogue. During the winter months the program turns to more formal entertainment when the curtain rises on a student theater. The stage is in the center of the establishment, and dinner theater productions are a special attraction at Max-Emanuel Brauerei. In addition to small theatrical plays, the *bühne* (stage) is lit for folk-music groups, variety acts and occasional amateur nights.

Max-Emanuel Brauerei is a beer garden and lokal that caters to a primarily young crowd. But like so many establishments in Munich, it attracts all age-groups and discriminates against none. All visitors are welcome here, and a trip to this beer garden in the center of the city's student quarter is a class worth making. Its report card shows 3-1/2 beers.

**Max-Emanuel's courtyard beer garden offers half- or full-liter mugs of beer.**

Munich's beer halls turn wild and crazy when rival soccer teams are in town.

Happy Hour takes on added zest at a local *Stammtisch.*

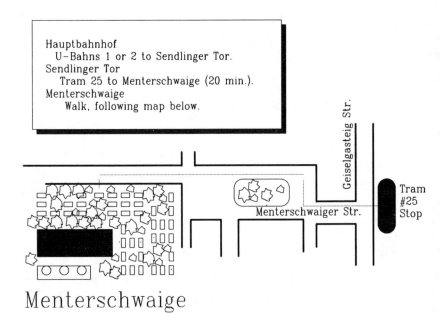

Hauptbahnhof
  U-Bahns 1 or 2 to Sendlinger Tor.
Sendlinger Tor
  Tram 25 to Menterschwaige (20 min.).
Menterschwaige
  Walk, following map below.

Geiselgasteig Str.

Menterschwaiger Str.

Tram
#25
Stop

# Menterschwaige

Menterschwaige
Menterschwaigstrasse 4
8000 Munich 90

(089) 640734/645465

Lowenbrau

11:30 a.m. to 11:30 p.m.

2100 in Beer Garden

# Menterschwaige

*O*nly in Munich would a beer garden play a role in that oldest of life's dramas: the eternal love triangle. And on a royal stage no less. Menterschwaige, today a favorite among Munich's beer garden frequenters, was once a part of the royal estate of King Ludwig I. Ludwig, you may remember, married Princess Therese von Sachsen-Hildburghausen in 1810 and gave the city the excuse it needed to launch the world's rowdiest keg party, Oktoberfest.

The marriage of the soon-to-be king and queen of Bavaria progressed swimmingly for awhile. But, the king's wandering eye eventually fell on the lovely image of the Spanish dancer Lola Montez and troubles began. The elicit love affair blossomed and when the queen got word of it, the lithe Lola was forced to leave town. Well, almost. Ludwig, still in the throes of his mid-life crisis, hid her away in a cathedral of his youth, the Menterschwaige.

Here in a hut the young Prince Ludwig had once reserved as a commune of sorts for befriended artisans and architects, dubbed the "Alt England", the king continued his nightly trysts with Lola. For a month the steamy romance played on. When the emotional fires dwindled, the Spanish

**A typical afternoon beer garden crowd fills the Menterschwaige.**

99

lady and the Bavarian monarch parted company.  Lola went on to a successful cabaret career.  For Ludwig, however, the relationship — which some still insist was only platonic — contributed to his downfall.  Despite his many architectural gifts to Munich and his kingdom, the monarch was besieged by public reprobation for his scandalous affair with Lola.  The final straw occurred when he tried to raise the price of beer.  His subjects might have forgiven a little royal infidelity, but never the attempt to pad the royal purse at the expense of their public brew.  Ludwig abdicated in 1848 and retired to his country estate to follow his true love as Munich's celebrated patron of the arts.

The romantic interlude of 150 years ago is today a curious footnote to the history of Menterschwaige.  The sprawling beer garden and restaurant exhibit little of their royal past.  The atmosphere is more of a traditional Munich establishment, with abundant shade from stands of mature chestnut trees sheltering rows of wood tables able to accommodate some 2,000 guests.  Most of the tables are uncovered, thus self-service is the rule.  The fast-food and grill stands offer an unusually wide variety of cooked meats, sausages and salads.  The portable crepe stand in the beer garden is a hint of the French influence seen on the menu inside the restaurant (the high prices are another clue).  A small courtyard serving area with linen-covered tables on the far side of the restaurant commonly hosts wedding receptions, private festivities and other more-formal affairs.

A well-designed and strategically located children's play area at a far end of the beer garden will keep the kiddies occupied.

Menterschwaige is what Münchners often refer to as a *Geheimtip*, a close-hold secret known only to the more enlightened and knowledgeable of the city's beer-drinking crowd.  And there are evidently plenty who are in on the secret.  On a warm weekend summer day the beer garden is full to overflowing with the locally rich and famous, as well as the well-represented middle class.  Menterschwaige is a little more upscale than most, and the prices inside the restaurant reflect that fact.  However, the real draw is the large beer garden where the cost of an afternoon is more reasonable.  The place has plenty of class and is always an excellent choice for a visit to a traditional Munich beer garden.  It's easy to see what attracted the King of Bavaria to this area — in addition to Lola Montez, of course.  It gets 4-1/2 beers.

A street entertainer plies his trade in Menterschwaige beer garden.

Hauptbahnhof
    U–Bahn 2 or 5 to Michaelibad
Michaelibad U–Bahn Stop
    Exit using escalator (not ramp) and
    follow bus sign – St. Michael Str.
    (Ostseite)
    Take bus 93 or 94 one stop to
    Heinrich–Wieland Str.
Heinrich–Wieland Str.
    Walk across street to beer garden.
Note:  this is on same route for
Franziskaner Garten (see write–up)

St. Viet Str.

Bus 94/95
Heinrich–
Wieland Str.

Heinrich Wieland Str.,

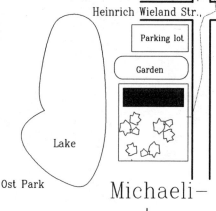

Parking lot

Garden

Lake

Ost Park

# Michaeli– garten

Michaeligarten
Feichtstrasse 10
8000 Munich 83

(089) 4316993

Lowenbrau

10 a.m. to 12 midnight

2000 in Beer Garden
250 on the Terrace
240 in Restaurant

# Michaeligarten

*M*ost of Munich's beer gardens have a history reaching back
several centuries. Their loyal patrons include several generations of families who have frequented the same establishment since *Opa* was
a teenager. Customers of Michaeligarten, on the other hand, might not be
old enough to vote. This beer garden in Munich's Ost (East) Park shatters
the mold by having secured its niche among the city's most popular
establishments in barely the time needed for the varnish to wear off the
wood. It is testament that a beer garden need not be old to be good. Real
good.

Built along with Munich's Ost park in 1973, Michaeligarten is a prize
of a beer garden with lots of neo-tradition. The foreground is a large (albeit
man-made) lake, with a fountain of water that sprays a continuous cascade.
The adjacent area is rolling green hills criss-crossed by walking paths that
roam throughout the park. It's a place where Münchners bring the entire
family on warm weekend afternoons, to let the kids play in the water or along
the shores of the lake.

Michaeligarten is made for relaxation. The lake and park setting is
enough to take 20 points off anyone's blood pressure. Since the blueprint
is totally self-service, the economics are much more in favor of the customers.
The large *Schmankerl* stand, with lots of flavorful Bavarian-style snacks, is
a cut above most fast-food-and-beer outlets. After an afternoon here and
enough to eat and drink, the impulse is to spread a blanket down by the lake
and check one's eyelids for holes.

Michaeligarten attracts large crowds but few tourists. It's a great find
and among the very best Munich has to offer, even if it is barely old enough
to drink. It gets 4-1/2 beers and a top recommendation.

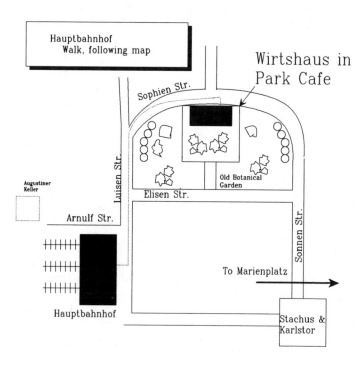

Hauptbahnhof
Walk, following map

Wirtshaus in
Park Cafe

Sophien Str.

Luisen Str.

Augustiner
Keller

Old Botanical
Garden

Elisen Str.

Arnulf Str.

Sonnen Str.

To Marienplatz

Hauptbahnhof

Stachus &
Karlstor

Park Cafe
Sophienstrasse 7
8000 Munich 2

(089) 598319

Lowenbrau

10 a.m. to 1 a.m.

1400 in Beer Garden
160 in Restaurant

# Park Cafe

$\mathcal{T}$ he century was just beginning and there was no finer nightclub in all of Munich than the Park Cafe. Gentlemen in tophats and tails and their ladies in chic evening gowns danced the night away on polished black marble floors below crystal chandeliers. Couples relaxed on stuffed velvet settees or gathered around the long mahogany bar to talk politics or the latest trends from Paris. Others strolled through the botanical gardens, just outside.

The velvet, marble, mahogany, and crystal are still there. The botanical gardens remain. But the luster of the Park Cafe's golden age is gone. In its place is a modern era of disco, funk, rap and soul with an appeal of its own. Hundreds of young customers still arrive — presumably sans chauffeured limo — on weekend evenings to dance to a different drummer well into the next morning. When the colored lights are flashing and the music blaring, one can only ponder whether the disco is holding the Park Cafe hostage, or the other way around.

The beer garden is another matter. Under separate management, the Park Cafe beer garden and restaurant is the Dr. Jekyll to the Mr. Hyde living next door. A logical addition to the city's Old Botanical Garden, the establishment holds the distinction as the closest beer emporium to the main train station, an important note for those in a hurry. The beer garden, smack in the middle of row after neat row of flowers and other botanical exhibits, has both service and self-serve sections (again, look for the tables that are covered). The kitchen stays open until 10 p.m. (the beer garden to 1 a.m.) and serves a limited assortment of dishes from a standard menu. The *Tagesschmankerl* menu insert offers daily specials and better deals for light inexpensive snacks.

The beer garden and nightclub live side by side in peaceful coexistence. Sitting in the beer garden after the disco heats up is much like being in someone's backyard with a frat party going on next door. The urge to get in on the action is hard to resist. Many an evening that begins in the shade of the beer garden ends at 4 a.m. on the black marble dance floor of the Park Cafe. Party crashers are welcome, but just remember to bring lots of money. Someone has to pay for all that mahogany panelling and velvet upholstering.

The Park Cafe, a unique blend of boisterous bistro and Bavarian beer garden, gets 3-1/2 beers.

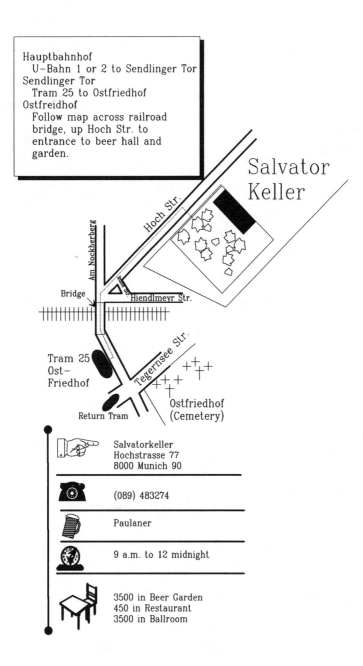

Hauptbahnhof
  U–Bahn 1 or 2 to Sendlinger Tor
Sendlinger Tor
  Tram 25 to Ostfriedhof
Ostfreidhof
  Follow map across railroad
  bridge, up Hoch Str. to
  entrance to beer hall and
  garden.

Salvator
Keller

Hoch Str.

Am Nockherberg

Bohn Str.

Bridge

Hiendlmeyr Str.

Tegernsee Str.

Tram 25
Ost–
Friedhof

+ + +
+ + +
+

Ostfriedhof
(Cemetery)

Return Tram

Salvatorkeller
Hochstrasse 77
8000 Munich 90

(089) 483274

Paulaner

9 a.m. to 12 midnight

3500 in Beer Garden
450 in Restaurant
3500 in Ballroom

# Salvator Keller

*L*egend has it that the Knights of Saint John spent all those centuries in search of the Holy Grail because it was filled with beer, "stark" beer. One trip to the Nockherberg—the hill overlooking the Isar and home to Salvator Keller — and one quickly learns what kept those ancient zealots busy on their fanatical quest. Salvator Keller is the principal outlet of the Salvator-Paulaner-Thomasbräu brewery next door. In addition to the well-regarded Paulaner brew, the world-famous Salvator dopple-bock strong beer is served here year-round. That may not seem like such a drawing card until one realizes that most other breweries in Munich — and throughout Germany for that matter — feature the seasonal strong beer only during a relatively short two-week period beginning around "Joseph's Day" on the 19th of March. This is the so-called *Starkbierzeit*, or strong beer time, when heavily-malted brews approaching 8 percent (vol.) alcohol are dispensed with impunity.

**Craziness abounds during Starkbierzeit (strong beer season) in Salvator Keller.**

The history of Salvator Keller is well integrated with its beer. Early in the 17th century, the Paulaner monks emigrated from Italy and established a monastery in Munich. Soon thereafter, in 1629, they brewed a special-occasions beer, dubbed Sankt Vaters Bier, or sacred father's brew, owing to its purported miraculous healing powers. Certainly, aches and pains were temporarily postponed under its influence, but the truth was, potency aside, the beer tasted lousy. That changed when Barnabas Still entered the Paulaner order a century or so later. Brother Barnabas, the son of a well-reputed local brewer, transformed the suds into something divine. By 1770, the beer — known simply around Munich by the slang-shortened "Salvator" name — was being widely dispensed. At a time when religious orders were heavily regulated by the secular authorities, Münchners found it easy to look the other way so long as the powerful brew kept flowing. Barnabas, certainly no fool, would take the trouble to keep the local duke, Karl Theodor, well supplied with his product. Finally, the by now well-oiled duke granted Paulaner Brothers, Inc. exclusive rights to freely market their beer on the 26th of February, 1780.

With secularization of the cloisters two decades later, the Paulaner brewery fell into private hands. In 1836, a brewer named Zacherl was able to petition King Ludwig I to break with tradition and allow the sale of strong beer to be moved up from April to the days just after the beginning of Lent (mid-February to first week in March). Thus, the stage was set for the Starkbier season, with Salvator leading the way.

The tradition survives, and Salvator is today widely imitated, but seldom duplicated. A search of local trade-

**The ultimate status symbol for a regular at Salvator Keller is a place of honor in the *Kruge Bank*.**

marks lists more than 120 registered strong beers, many of which borrow the -ator suffix to advertise their added vigor. They range from the better known copy-cat brews (for some reason "Imitator" is not one of the 120) such as Triumphator, Optimator, Delicator, Maximator and Animator, to the lesser known but nevertheless graphic, Vitamator, Sufficator, Multiplicator and Raritator.

The era of today's Salvator Keller began on May 1, 1899 when the restaurant was renovated and expanded, offering a full menu and "cellar-cooled" beer. The complex features six *Stüben* (small bars) with seating for 600; three large banquet halls or ballrooms to hold up to 2,000; a beer garden with seating for 3,500. Next to the Hofbräuhaus, this is the best known among Munich's beer palaces.

The Salvator Keller is like a magnet during Starkbier time, attracting thousands of locals to answer the "call of the Berg" and join in festivities that resemble a corner Oktoberfest. On normal days, the place is filled with armies of brewery workers imbibing their own day's hard work.

When the sun is shining, an early afternoon arrival is recommended to insure seat availability in the beer garden. Waiter or waitress service is available at the tables with table cloths; the rest are self-service (*selbstbedienung*). Salvator Keller serves half-liters to 2 p.m. in the beer garden. After that, full liters are served on a one-size-fits-all basis.

A Munich mainstay that gets inexplicably snubbed by outsiders, Salvator Keller should be high on the list as a beer hall and beer garden with lots of tradition and age-blackened-wood atmosphere. It is an outstanding selection any time of year. Its commodious interior makes it especially amenable to an off-season visit (such as during the strong beer festival) when foul-weather plans are in order. Salvator Keller earns 4 industrial strength beers.

Hautpbahnhof
  U-Bahn 1 or 2 to Sendlinger Tor
Sendlinger Tor
  U-Bahn 6 to Studentenstadt
Studentenstadt
  Bus **37** two stops to Sankt Emmerams
Sankt Emmerams Bus Stop
  Follow Map Below

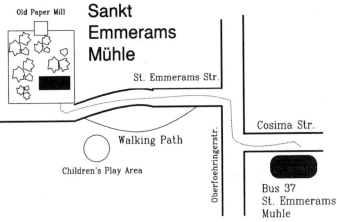

Sankt Emmerams Muhle
St. Emmeram 41
8000 Munich 81

(089) 953971

Spaten−Brau

11 a.m. to 10 p.m.

1200 in Beer Garden
180 in Restaurant

# Sankt Emmerams Mühle

$\mathcal{N}$ ot the river but the stream . . . down by the old Sankt Emmerams Mühle. Anybody who is somebody, and everybody who is anybody at one time or another can count themselves among the patrons of this diamond among Munich's rural beer garden treasures. Lifestyles of the rich and famous converge daily with the workaday existence of the city's middle-class multitudes at the one-time paper mill-turned-restaurant and beer garden near the Isar River.

Historically, the Sankt Emmerams locale is connected with the city's founding. In 1158, King Henry the Lion destroyed a nearby toll bridge over the Isar at Oberföhring that had been a lucrative venture of his rich royal uncle. He built his own money-making crossing a few miles upstream at a village called Munichen. The city was thus chartered as a consequence of Henry's medieval entrepreneurship.

"The Mill of Saint Emmerams" was in existence in the 14th century. The mill stayed busy — first with the conversion of grains and later production of paper — for several hundred years. As a sideline, the mill management began serving food and beverages to customers in 1825 by

**A walking and bicycle trail borders the beer garden and meanders through the countryside.**

The old paper mill, still standing, behind the beer garden.

converting adjacent offices and waiting rooms into a restaurant and outdoor beer garden. The mill and restaurant were reconstructed in 1866 in the style they appear today. When the milling business ground to a halt after World War I, the gastronomical side of the house took over.

The current proprietor or *wirt* has taken painstaking care to preserve the restaurant's centuries-old atmosphere. With a devotion to detail, he has used 19th-century timbers and other antique building materials to make needed interior renovations. The result is an unspoiled, living museum piece that has become almost as famous as the entourage of big name entertainers and film stars who visit here.

Sankt Emmerams' guest book reads like a Who's Who of international celebrities. ABBA, Led Zepplin, Tina Turner, Rod Stewart, and Donna Summer have all paused for a brew in the shady beer garden. Famous film personalities like the late William Holden, Stephanie Powers, and the late Lee Marvin are listed among its notable customers. The Bavarian political king himself, Franz Joseph Strauss, once held court here. But most patrons of Sankt Emmerams Mühle don't come to see or be

The short walk from the tram stop to Sankt Emmerams Mühle passes this old country chapel.

seen. Most are everyday Münchners who arrive on foot or by bicycle, after a walk or ride along one of the many scenic pathways that meander through the countryside and terminate at the far side of the beer garden. They bring their own food and spread their own tablecloths and are not intimidated by any luminary sitting nearby. Thus it is with Munich's beer gardens, where several hundred years of custom and tradition have created the ultimate classless society. When every seat is the same, the best seat in the house is the one that is available. And the celebrity is the one who gets there first.

The pinnacle quality of food, beverage, and service at Sankt Emmerams Mühle is enough to make every customer feel like a VIP, and at a price a commoner can afford. The wirt has seen to that and has created a rare experience that shouldn't be missed. The country inn atmosphere in a setting of rolling hills, and grassy meadows is without equal. Sankt Emmerams Mühle justly deserves the reputation it has earned of being among Munich's very best. It gets an unqualified 5 full beers!

**The beer garden at Sankt Emmerams Mühle.**

# Schiess statte

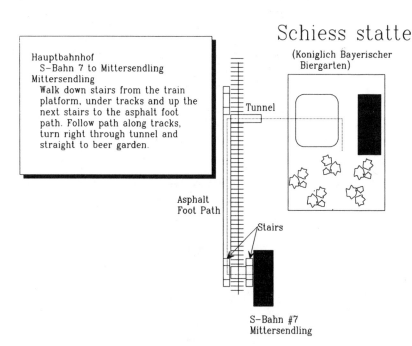

(Koniglich Bayerischer Biergarten)

Hauptbahnhof
  S-Bahn 7 to Mittersendling
Mittersendling
  Walk down stairs from the train
  platform, under tracks and up the
  next stairs to the asphalt foot
  path. Follow path along tracks,
  turn right through tunnel and
  straight to beer garden.

Tunnel

Asphalt
Foot Path

Stairs

S-Bahn #7
Mittersendling

Schiess statte
Zielstattstrasse 6
8000 Munich 70

(089) 786940

Kaltenberger Brau

11 a.m. to 10 p.m.

2500 in Beer Garden
300 in Restaurant

# Schießstätte
### (Königlich Bayerische Biergarten)

*M* unich's beer gardens seldom change their names. Owners may come and go, but the name recognition built up over centuries is fervently protected. Thus, when the Königlich Bayerische Biergarten came under new management several years ago, it kept the old moniker, but added a new one, Schießstätte. Take your pick. You'll find both names in the phonebook. Whatever you call it, Schießstätte (the lesser mouthful) is both beautiful and spacious. The 2,500-seat beer garden has been designed with about half the anchored wooden tables in the shade of 100-year-old chestnut trees and the rest in the open for those who want to take in some late-season rays before fall turns to winter. The restaurant is housed in a Victorian-style mansion at one end of the beer garden. It is also home to the region's largest marksman and sport-shooting club, thus helping to explain the recent name change (*schießen* means to shoot in German).

The local wirt is proud of the Kaltenberger Beer he serves and its history. Prince Leopold, a Wittelsbach ruler, established the Kaltenberg palace brewery several hundred years ago and the suds served the royal family in some unusual ways. Next to the salt tax, income generated by the royal brewing business kept the House of Wittelsbach in deep sauerkraut for many years. On the "medicinal" side, Duke Emanuel drank a full liter of beer every noon and evening for his entire healthy life. The strangest use of the suds occurred in 1823 when the Bavarian national theater caught fire. Cold winter temperatures froze the local water supply and the fire was eventually doused, you guessed it, with beer. Maximilian I, a bit of an ingrate, later rebuilt the national theater with money raised by hiking the beer tax.

The Kaltenberger beer at Schießstätte-a/k/a Königlich Bayerische Biergarten is as tasty as the better-known brands and cheaper than most. The food selections from the restaurant or the beer garden's outdoor snack bar also lean to the reasonable side. In fact, everything about this establishment is easy on the pocketbook with no compromise in the quality or service. The business is active in promoting seasonal fare, including special programs during the March strong beer season and a Bavarian folk theater that performs from middle October to the end of March*. The crowd on weekends is large and strains the capacity of this community meeting place. Families are especially at home here. The food and drink are a bargain and the atmosphere is comfortable and friendly. Call it what you will — Schießstätte or Königlich Bayerische Biergarten — it's well worth your visit. Together they get 4 beers.

---

*The Millionendorf-Theater operates mid-Oct. to end of March with Fri. and Sat. night performances starting at 8 p.m. (doors open at 6:30 p.m. when the band begins). Tel. for reservations and ticket information is 760-1113 or 714-6031. Tickets for the strong beer season activities can be obtained at the same numbers.

# Siebenbrunn

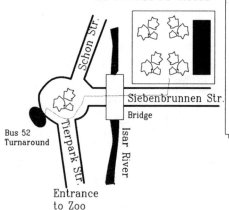

Hauptbahnhof
    U-Bahn to Marienplatz
Marienplatz
    Follow bus (not tram) sign
    and exit for Bus 52 for
    Tierpark. Take bus to final
    stop at Tierpark (zoo).
Tierpark
    Walk, following map.

Note: Continue on Siebenbrunnen Str. up hill
to Harlichinger Einkehr restaurant and beer
garden. See write-up/map on Harlichinger
Einkehr.

Siebenbrunn
Siebenbrunner Strasse 5
8000 Munich 90

(089) 650848

Spaten-Brau

10 a.m. to 11 p.m.

800 in Beer Garden
140 in Restaurant

# Siebenbrunn

*G*rab the kids and head for the zoo. And after the kiddies have dragged you through several miles of four-legged exhibits from six continents, wouldn't a tall cool one go good right now? As luck would have it, a short detour from Munich's zoo entrance is Siebenbrunn, one of the city's more attractive beer gardens.

Siebenbrunn ("Seven Springs") was there long before any nearby zoological undertaking. In the 18th century the area was a part of the royal hunting preserves of Bavarian Duke Karl Albrecht. In 1732, another avid royal huntsman, Baron von Preysing, sent his emissary in search of a suitable location for overnight resting of the royal hunting nags. Siebenbrunn, with plenty of running water and nearby game — albeit belonging to someone else — seemed an ideal stopover point. So, the baron's people got with the duke's people and struck up a 60-day temporary lease agreement, one assumes with some option for renewal. The prototypical time-share plan was followed by an early example of squatters rights. Suddenly, Siebenbrunn was under new management and stables were erected on the site.

The normal evolution prevailed, and the spirit of the hunt was replaced by other spirits, most notably those sold across the bar of the local country tavern. The horse barn was turned into a restaurant of sorts, and one can imagine the natural incentive to develop an area with lots of outdoor seating.

Historical records reveal the ownership dispute was settled by 1763 when the property was officially sold to a count with the prophetic name of Maximilian von Baumgarten (literally "tree garden"). For a time the whole complex was pressed into service as a cottage factory turning out sandals and boots. The sole of the business wore thin, and by the early 19th century Siebenbrunn was back to being a lokal and beer garden again.

Siebenbrunn has survived floods (1899) and bombs (1944) and thousands of tourists on safari. It's an excellent example of a traditional Munich beer garden. The lush vegetation in the surrounding area provides plenty of summer shade and atmosphere. Although the restaurant is small, it serves up an ample selection of typical Bavarian dishes. The real treat is the beer garden and the proximity to the Hellabrunn Tierpark or zoo. Siebenbrunn is a perfect day-trip for the kids, but you don't have to answer the call of the wild to make the trip worthwhile. It gets 3-1/2 beers.

(Note: A tandem visit to nearby Harlachinger Einkehr is made by walking up the hill. See map and information on Harlachinger Einkehr.)

Hauptbahnhof
  S-Bahn 7 to Harras
Harras
  Tram 26 two stops to Herzog
  Ernzt Platz, passing beer garden
  on left.
Herzog Ernzt Platz
  Follow map back to beer garden.

Tram 26
Herzog-Ernzt
Platz

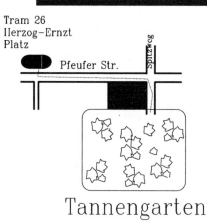

Pfeufer Str.

# Tannengarten

Tannengarten
Pfeuferstrasse 32
8000 Munich 70

(089) 771900

Hacker-Pschorr Brau

9:30 a.m. to 1 a.m.
Closed Mondays

800 in Beer Garden
70 in Restaurant
250 in Banquet Room

# *Tannengarten*

S o where are they? A *Tannengarten* without the *Tannenbäume?* "That's just it," says the wirt, as though letting you in on the joke for the first time. "A pine garden without any pines! Don't you get it?" Frankly, no, but that's all right. Tannengarten does fine without them. This corner beer garden and restaurant-lokal isn't hurting for shade, thanks to a stand of mature, fully foliated chestnut trees. It's not lacking for customers either. With a full century behind it (est. 1889), Tannengarten has won over the local neighborhood with a combination of good food, courteous service and cold Hacker-Pschorr beer.

Tannengarten is a durable institution in the Sendlinger section of Munich. Local chroniclers note that the historically significant "farmers revolt" of 1705 took place around the corner. A December parade winding through the neighborhood is held in honor of the revolutionary event and a painting depicting the battle hangs in Tannengarten's banquet room.

Of more recent historical vintage, the backyard beer garden harkens back to a time when loyalties were drawn along streetside boundaries and families identified with the communities where they grew up. As was the custom in Germany a century ago, the church and the local *bierkeller* shared responsibility as neighborhood magnets for the area's social activities. The church, just down the street, and Tannengarten are still packing them in. The beer garden continues to do its part by sponsoring a number of local *vereins* or clubs that serve both a social and recreational function. Community choirs and sports and athletic clubs, amateur orchestras and brass bands all call Tannengarten home. A Bavarian folk theater group stages monthly *Bayerischer abends* October through March.

Along with whatever timely entertainment the social calendar might bring, Tannengarten is always good for plenty of traditional outdoor beer garden enjoyment and tasty Bavarian food specialties. One of the more noteworthy dishes is *Schweinnenacken auf Wildschweinart.* This "hunter's-style" meal is made from pork soaked in spiced red wine for four days and then simmered in a stew of onions, celery, and carrots. The delectable result is a little like German *Sauerbraten,* only better. It's one of many gourmet-style dishes that makes this as good a place to eat as it is to enjoy a refreshing beer.

Tannengarten is a quaint, comfortable suburban beer garden. Unpretentious and unassuming, it is a bit of *alltag* (everyday) Munich and an unfettered view of local customs and tradition. It gets 3 beers.

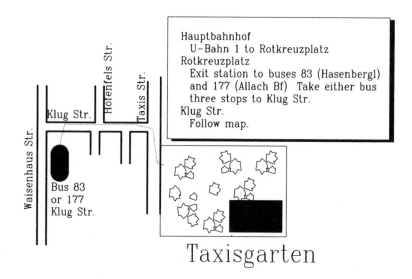

Hauptbahnhof
  U–Bahn 1 to Rotkreuzplatz
Rotkreuzplatz
  Exit station to buses 83 (Hasenbergl)
  and 177 (Allach Bf)  Take either bus
  three stops to Klug Str.
Klug Str.
  Follow map.

Klug Str.

Hofenfels Str.

Taxis Str.

Waisenhaus Str.

Bus 83
or 177
Klug Str.

Taxisgarten

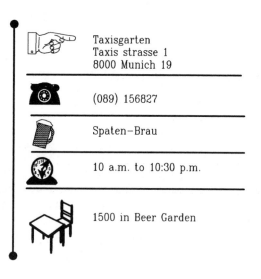

Taxisgarten
Taxis strasse 1
8000 Munich 19

(089) 156827

Spaten–Brau

10 a.m. to 10:30 p.m.

1500 in Beer Garden

# Taxisgarten

*G*ermany's martial past is legion. There are few countries in the world whose citizens are more sensitive to a record of two world wars in the space of a century, and many thousands of casualties that were taken on all sides during the conflicts. The fabric of collective guilt has been woven through this republic. Today's Germany, economically strong and reunited, has outlived its warrior past and is foremost among western democracies in both its abhorrence to war and its regard for peace. Yet the reminders remain, even in its beer gardens.

Taxisgarten, established in 1920, was dedicated to the rehabilitation of wounded veterans of World War I. The enterprise was originally the property of the *Vereins Kriegs- und Körperbeschädigte* (Association of War-wounded) and served as a social gathering point for those whose service would forever bear the scars of war. The bonds of national sacrifice were strong and Taxisgarten's patronage remained exclusively former military. A building to house the association was constructed. And, in one of history's tragic ironies, the entire complex — structures and beer garden — was consumed during the century's second conflagration, World War II.

Post-war rebuilding was accompanied by a rejection of all things bellicose and belligerent. The organization of war veterans opened its doors to the neighborhood and Taxisgarten became a quiet haven for conversations dominated less by war stories than the mundane issues of the day. The restaurant and beer garden were completely renovated in 1988. The last remaining memorial to its martial origins is seen over the restaurant entry way. The overhead portal relief displays a helmeted German soldier accompanied by an inscription. The word *opfer* is used, which in German can mean either "sacrifice" or "victim". The semantical contradiction is left to speak for itself. Taxisgarten fits much better the peaceful mold. The shady, 1,500-seat beer garden is a neighborhood mainstay and a green oasis

in a residential surrounding of stairwell apartments and onion-domed churches. The *speisekarte* or menu features the standard selection of roasted chicken, pork shank, and meaty spareribs. Fresh-baked pretzels are also a local favorite, along with plenty of Bavarian-style snacks.

The beer garden draws from a local crowd of young professionals, families and an entourage of students. This is a prime example of a Munich beer garden that relies on a loyal patronage encouraged by a conscious management effort to provide both quality and service. Taxisgarten gets 3-1/2 beers.

**Portal display at Taxisgarten.**

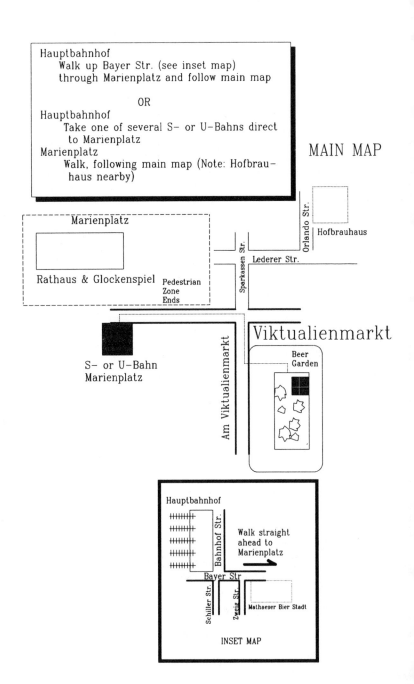

Hauptbahnhof
    Walk up Bayer Str. (see inset map)
    through Marienplatz and follow main map

                    OR
Hauptbahnhof
    Take one of several S- or U-Bahns direct
    to Marienplatz
Marienplatz
    Walk, following main map (Note: Hofbrau-
    haus nearby)

MAIN MAP

Orlando Str.

Hofbrauhaus

Marienplatz

Rathaus & Glockenspiel

Pedestrian
Zone
Ends

Sparkassen Str.

Lederer Str.

S- or U-Bahn
Marienplatz

Am Viktualienmarkt

Viktualienmarkt

Beer
Garden

Hauptbahnhof

Bahnhof Str.

Walk straight
ahead to
Marienplatz

Bayer Str

Schiller Str.

Zweig Str.

Mathaeser Bier Stadt

INSET MAP

122

# Biergarten Viktualienmarkt

*T*his is a place best visited on a Saturday morning or early afternoon. That's when the weekly Viktualienmarkt, the city's central food market, is in full swing. Everything from *Suppe* to *Nuß* and a million other daily necessities (as in victuals) are hawked here. It's where Münchners come to shop 'til they drop — or, rather, stop to enjoy a Maß of refreshing beer.

Viktualienmarkt, a Munich tradition since 1807, is no touristy museum piece. It's a living, thriving activity. The Saturday morning ritual of bartering, haggling, and buying has changed little in the past two hundred years. A colorful display of wares from all over Germany and Europe attests to Munich having served as a southern and northern European trade center for centuries.

The beer garden is wedged in the market's middle, in the center of a ring of flower, fresh fruit, vegetable, meat and other produce stands. Although marked by a towering May Pole, the beer garden is anything but hard to find. The greatest concentration of people is there, and seats are at a premium. Numerous food stands and outdoor restaurants are a part of the market complex. Helping yourself to nearby food selections and smuggling them back to your seat in the beer garden is no crime.

Interspersed among the beer garden patrons is a series of statues commemorating Munich's six most popular folk singers and comedians. The fountain figures represent Karl Valentin (1882-1948) and his partner Liesl Karlstadt (1892-1960). Also enshrined in permanent bronze are the comedians Weiss Ferdl (1883-1949) and Ida Schumacher (1895-1956), the singer Roider Jackl (1906-1975), and actress Elise Aulinger (1881-1965).

Viktualienmarkt
Am Viktualienmarkt 6
8000 Munich 2

(089) 297545

Alle Munchner

9 a.m. to 10 p.m.
Closed Sun. & Holidays

500 in Beer Garden

It's hard to separate the beer garden and the market. And they probably shouldn't be. That also means that when the Saturday-morning-to-afternoon market is ended, the beer garden is just another pretty place. When the market is on, Biergarten Viktualienmarkt gets 3 beers. When it's off . . .

Hauptbahnhof
  S-7 to Harras
Harras
  Exit S-Bahn station on Meindl Str.
  (picture of a tram). Take Tram 26
  to last stop, Lorettoplatz.
Lorettoplatz
  Follow map. Beergarden is
  about 1/4 mile walk in woods.

# Waldheim

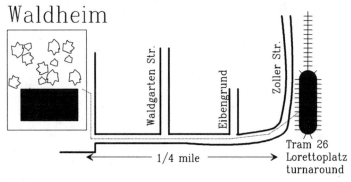

1/4 mile → Tram 26
Lorettoplatz
turnaround

Waldheim
Zum Waldheim 1
8000 Munich 70

(089) 7146288

Hacker-Pschorr-Brau

10 a.m. to 11 p.m.
Closed on Mondays

1000 in Biergarten
400 in Ballroom
80 in Restaurant

# Waldheim

*T* hose who enjoy the outdoors and don't mind following bread crumbs back to the hotel, should make the trip to Waldheim. Although only about a quarter-mile from the nearest tram stop, this small beer garden and restaurant is at the edge of Munich's wooded outback. The Waldheim, or "forest home" is true to its name. It must be the place where Hansel and Gretel, in search of the sinister Gingerbread House, stopped off for a quick beer.

The crowd tends to be over thirty and not afraid to mix it up, as evidenced by the weekly Sunday afternoon (3 p.m. start) *Tanztee*, literally "dance tea". The name is a little misleading, because beer, not tea, is the staple drink, and nobody sits around munching on cookies while the disco is in full swing. The beer garden seems to be a meeting place for older singles and nomadic bands of naturelovers who spend their weekends in the woods.

Table service is the rule throughout the beer garden and no picnic baskets are allowed. The inexpensive food is outstanding and the service fast and friendly.

Waldheim is at a major crossroads for a series of hiking and bicycle trails that wind through the woods. Thus, it's an ideal lokal for those who like to spend time enjoying the natural side of things. Few beer gardens in Munich are so secluded and yet have this much to offer. A little bit off the beaten path, but a great choice for those who like to walk, Waldheim gets 3 beers.

Hauptbahnhof
  S-Bahn 7 to Grosshesselohe/Isartalbf
Grosshesselohe/Isartalbf
  Visit station brewery.  Walk, following
  map.

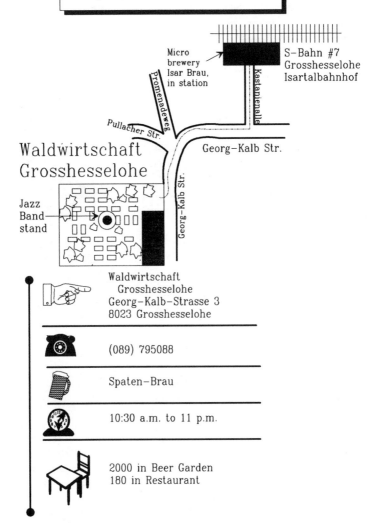

Micro
brewery
Isar Brau,
in station

Promenadeweg

Kastanienalle

S-Bahn #7
Grosshesselohe
Isartalbahnhof

Pullacher Str.

Georg-Kalb Str.

Waldwirtschaft
Grosshesselohe

Georg-Kalb Str.

Jazz
Band
stand

Waldwirtschaft
    Grosshesselohe
Georg-Kalb-Strasse 3
8023 Grosshesselohe

(089) 795088

Spaten-Brau

10:30 a.m. to 11 p.m.

2000 in Beer Garden
180 in Restaurant

# Waldwirtschaft Großhesselohe

*W*aldwirtschaft Großhesselohe is a mix of the best of old German tradition and modern day musical enjoyment. Nestled high atop a hillside overlooking the Isar Valley, "Wa-Wi" (pronounced Vah-Vee) as locals fondly refer to it is today center stage for some of the liveliest jazz and Big Band sounds in all of Bavaria. Everyday during summer months visitors to the garden and restaurant are treated to musical programs by bands from all over Europe, even Polish and Czech ensembles whose contemporary sounds belie their eastern origins. But don't let the modernity of the music fool you. This beer dispensary has roots reaching back hundreds of years.

The "Schweiger Hesselohe" was mentioned in official proclamations as early as 776, when it was listed as a region under control of the Bavarian Duke Tassilos. The first beer tavern was established in the 15th century and business has been fermenting steadily ever since. In 1779 a new wrinkle was added in the form of a farmer's market, which attracted more visitors and more customers for the foamy brew. Around 1800, a dance pavilion was

**Regular live jazz and Big-Band programs are a special attraction at "Wa-Wi".**

127

established, and along with it the Waldwirtschaft name. The place became an instant hit with Munich's young crowd who at last had a place to meet where, one would imagine, the beer was cold but the romance was not.

In 1852 the railroad reached Großhesselohe. With customers now arriving by the carload, history records that on a good day 10,000 visitors staggered down the slopes of the Waldwirtschaft. A high-water mark was reached on Easter Sunday 1900 when some 11 thousand liters of beer were dispensed — still a local record.

The Spaten Brewery, which itself had been around since 1397, bought the Waldwirtschaft Großhesselohe in 1930, thus fulfilling a long-awaited dream of the brewery's patriarchal Sedlmayr family. It was Gabriel Sedlmayr's dying wish of a century earlier to someday have the Wa-Wi as one of his own. The beer must have been flowing freely in that Big Beer Garden in the Sky the day they brought this one into the fold.

The restaurant and beer garden today are patterned around the celebrated "jazz" musical blueprint that gives the Wa-Wi its individuality. Tables, benches and chairs radiate from the center bandstand like spokes on a wheel. Benches line the beer garden's outer edge, affording visitors a breathtaking view of the lush, green Isartal river valley below. Well-foliated chestnut trees provide abundant shade throughout, and a children's play area in one corner keeps the small-fry engrossed while the adults enjoy a cool

**A horse-drawn carriage awaits the newlyweds at a reception in the beer garden.**

beer and food selections from the several *Schmankerl* stands nearby.

The Waldwirtschaft Großhesselohe boasts an excellent in-door/outdoor restaurant for more formal dining, featuring a wide selection of traditional Bavarian dishes.

All this and jazz music, too, is almost more than one could ask. A bonus, though, in that most of the summer help are Irish or English exchange students and workers, thus the mother tongue is all that's needed in getting exactly what you want, when you want it.

It doesn't get any better than this, and Waldwirtschaft Großhesselohe weighs in with a top 5-beer rating!

Note: The nearby train station arrival point (below) offers an unusual and refreshing diversion, since it has been recently refurbished into one of Munich's growing number of micro-breweries. The brew, manufactured on the premises, is a type of *weizen*, or wheat beer. Isar Brau's combination restaurant and small outdoor platform cafe also offers Hofbräuhaus brand libations for those who prefer the more familiar *helles* style of beer. Prelude to a visit to Wa-Wi should include a brief tour of this facility's glass-enclosed polished copper brewing plant. The cleanliness throughout is an encouraging introduction to the patently Bavarian art of brewing.

Hauptbahnhof
S-Bahn 1 to Freising (about a 30-minute ride)

Freising
Following map, walk from bahnhof across river to center of town.
Then walk down Vottinger Str. for about 3/4 of a mile. There are
signs leading to Weihenstephan along the way. Turn left at the
Sparkasse (bank). Walk up the hill to the Braustuberl and beer
garden.

Note: There is a bus at the bottom of the hill that runs to the train station. However, the
schedule is sporadic. Walking may still be the best alternative.

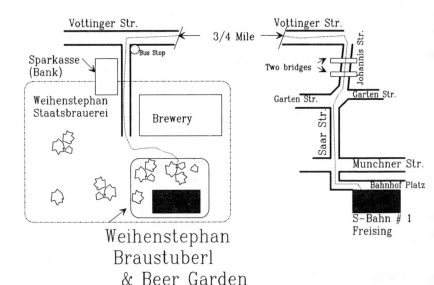

Weihenstephan
Braustuberl
& Beer Garden

# *Weihenstephan*

*W*eihenstephan is one of the oldest still-operating breweries in the world. Whether it's *the* oldest is a matter for historical purists to decide. Local literature holds that the monastery brewery was operational in 1040 as the very first outlet under the auspices of those world-famous Benedictine Brothers. And if that is true, then Weihenstephan certainly qualifies as the most senior among suds producers. But there is no written record that the brewery was able to actually sell its beer publicly, an important distinction.

The earliest documented account holds that Bishop Otto von Freising granted the Weihenstephan monks that right in 1146. Nevertheless, sometime between 725 when the Weihenstephan Cloister was founded and the mid 12th century when it was granted or renewed distribution rights, the monastery became well-versed in the manufacture of Munich's most durable product.

Secularization of the ecclesiastical breweries in 1803 was only the beginning for Weihenstephan. When the Bavarian government took control of this and some 200 other cloister breweries they also saw to the temporal side of business by establishing schools to advance the brewing arts. In 1852 a brewing curriculum was begun at the former Benedictine Abbey. By 1930 it was a full-fledged "college" under Munich University, and remains so today.

| | |
|---|---|
| 👉 | Weihenstephan<br>Weihenstephan 1<br>8050 Freising |
| ☎ | (08161) 13004 or 5 |
| 🍺 | Weihenstephan, brewed on premises |
| 🕘 | 9 a.m. to 11 p.m. |
| 🪑 | 500 in Beer Garden<br>500 in Restaurant |

Hardly a class teaching project, the state-run and university-affiliated operation is today a modern brewing plant in every way. During a one-hour tour of the facilities, the public is shown a modern, state-of-the art brewery where 40,000 gallons of beer are produced daily. Nine different types are brewed, all available for sampling in the shaded *Bräustüberl* (beer garden and restaurant) at the top of the hill.

The beer garden is small but comfortable and offers a view of the rolling grassy hills that make up the brewery grounds. The restaurant serves typical Bavarian dishes at a more than reasonable price. In fact, this beer garden is one of the most affordable anywhere, attesting to the generous state subsidies that keep prices within range of the limited budgets of the students who are enrolled here. With an eye toward promotional marketing, the brewery's well-stocked souvenir shop sells mugs, coasters, T-shirts and other Weihenstephan memorabilia at give-away prices.

The primary drawback is the relative lack of frequent, nearby public transportation (a bus from the train station runs sporadically) and the fact that Freising is the northernmost point of the Munich S-bahn line. Thus a trip to Weihenstephan can consume the better part of a morning in travel time. Those who enjoy learning more about brewing and the chance to tour an operating plant will gain the most from a visit. In all cases, the luxury of available time without the pressures of a tight schedule (allow a full day) will make the trip worthwhile. Those in a rush should look for more convenient beer-drinking venues. Weihenstephan rates 3-1/2 beers.

The "world's oldest brewery" offers one-hour tours, Monday through Thursday, on a reserved basis. The brewery prefers groups of 15 or more but will accommodate individuals in conjunction with full groups where possible. All tours must begin before 2 p.m. and can be reserved by calling the brewery at least a week in advance at 08161-3021. Cost for the tour is DM 3 for adults, children under 12 are free.

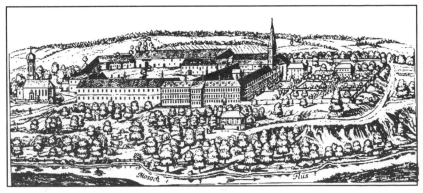

**Weihenstephan Cloister, prior to secularization.**

Brewers in Germany have been held in high esteem for centuries and awarded their own coat of arms (upper left). Brewing in Bavaria was first undertaken by ecclesiastical beer makers, as depicted (above) in the medieval drawing from 1430 (the oldest representation of a German brew master). The six-pointed star shown above and in the 1730 copper engraving left is yet another historical symbol of the beer-making art.

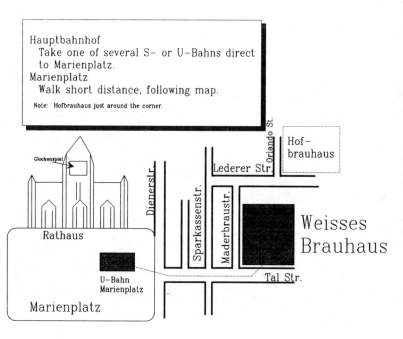

Hauptbahnhof
  Take one of several S- or U-Bahns direct
  to Marienplatz.
Marienplatz
  Walk short distance, following map.

Note: Hofbrauhaus just around the corner.

Glockenspiel

Hof-
brauhaus

Orlando St.

Lederer Str.

Dienerstr.

Sparkassenstr.

Maderbraustr.

Weisses
Brauhaus

Rathaus

U-Bahn
Marienplatz

Tal Str.

Marienplatz

Weisses Brauhaus
Tal Str. 10
8000 Munich 2

(089) 299875

Schneider Weisse
Karmeliten Kloster Urtyp

9 a.m. to 11:30 p.m.

400
in Restaurant

# Weisses Bräuhaus

S traight through the Marienplatz, just past the end of the pedestrian zone on the historic Tal Strasse, is the Weisses Bräuhaus. The name signals both the long history of this establishment as a former brewery and also the featured brew, Schneider Weissbier. The Tal Strasse was along a major trade route during the middle ages, leading from Salzburg to Augsburg. The adjacent street, Maderbräugasse, is named after an old Munich brewing family who plied their trade in the area for centuries. The building that houses Weisses Bräuhaus was a brewery as early as 1540 and probably for decades before that.

In 1872, Georg Schneider bought out the Maderbräu brewery and turned from the traditional lagers to producing a wheat or *weizen* beer, often called *weiss* or "white" beer. Thus, the Weisses in this case refers to the brew and not the exterior chalk-colored facade.

Schneider had earned his brewing spurs running the Weisses Hofbräuhaus around the corner, where the present-day Hofbräuhaus is located. He was able to turn both Maderbräu and the associated guest house into a thriving business. Eventually, the brewery had to move, but the beer restaurant and lokal stayed on.

The Weisses Bräuhaus today is especially popular among students and others who pause for a beer or a sumptuous meal before or after a trip to the Hofbräuhaus. The atmosphere here is busy, but not hectic. The food is outstanding and plentiful, including house specialties of roasted pork and beefshank, and various grilled sausages. It's not a bad idea to do as the locals do and catch your breath and a good meal at the Weisses Bräuhaus before wading into the Hofbräuhaus around the corner. Weisses Brauhaus, with one of the best menus in Munich, earns 3 beers.

# After Hours

$\mathcal{M}$ unich is a city that swings all night. While most beer halls and beer gardens close around midnight, a number of nightclubs and dance halls are just cranking up. They keep the lights burning, the music blaring and the beer flowing until the sun comes up. A taxi will take you there and a well-padded pocket book will let you stay awhile. After hours bars and discos in Munich are expensive and cover or entrance charges are the norm. It's not unusual for drink prices to double after the clock strikes 12. Be forewarned that doormen will sometimes deny entrance to those not meeting the prevailing dress codes or representative age groups. Still, these late-night bistros and clubs offer a "no-last-call" alternative for tireless beer-drinkers who can party with the roosters and still soar with the eagles in the morning. Here's a list of the best:

**Aquarius**
Leopoldstraße 194 (Munich 40)
Tel: 340-971
Hours: 9 p.m.-4 a.m.
Disco-dancing in Holiday Inn.

**Charly M**
Maximiliansplatz 5 (Munich 2)
Tel: 595-277
Hours: 9 p.m.-4 a.m.
Disco bar, over 30 crowd.

**Hotel Bayerischer Hof Nightclub**
Promenadeplatz 6 (Munich 2)
Tel: 212-00
Hours: 10:30 p.m.-3 a.m.
Live dance bands,
 international atmosphere,
 older crowd.

**Club Bavaria im Hilton Hotel**
Am Tucherpark 7 (Munich 22)
Tel: 384-50
Hours: 9 p.m.-3 a.m.
International dance bands,
older crowd.

**Fregatte**
Sonnestraße 17 (Munich 2)
Tel: 595-600
Hours: 10 p.m.-4 a.m.
Live and DJ dance music, young
crowd.

**Cabane-Bar**
Theresienstraße 40 (Munich 40)
Tel: 283-134
Hours: 9 p.m.-3 a.m.
Conversation, famous drinks.

**Cadillac**
Theklastraße 1 (Munich 2)
Tel: 266-974
Hours: 9 p.m.-4 a.m.
Disco Funk and Soul music.

**Harry's New York Bar**
Falkenturmstraße 9 (Munich 22)
Tel: 222-700
Hours: 4 p.m.-3 a.m., closed Sundays. Meeting place; not Paris but still world-famous bar, filled with "beautiful people". Around corner from HBHaus.

## Jet Dancing

Sendlinger Straße 55  (Munich 2)
Tel:  260-3987
Hours:  8 p.m.-2 a.m.
Airline theme, dance contests,
mixed crowd.

## Lenbach-Palast

Lenbachplatz 3  (Munich 2)
Tel:  595-080
Hours:  9 p.m.-4 a.m.
Plenty of glitz, live dance band,
mixed crowd.

## Maximilians

Maximiliansplatz 16  (Munich 2)
Tel:  223-252
Hours:  9 p.m.-3 a.m.,
closed Mondays
Yuppie disco, well-balanced
both sexes.

## Mirage

Am Kosttor 12  (Munich 2)
Tel:  226-661
Hours:  10 p.m.-4 a.m.
"New-Wave" Disco, young crowd.

## Nachtcafe

Maximiliansplatz 5  (Munich 2)
Tel:  595-900
Hours:  7 p.m.-5 a.m.
50s atmosphere, live listening
music.

## Park Cafe

Sophienstraße 7  (Munich 2)
Tel:  598-313
Hours:  10 p.m.-4 a.m.
Century-old nightclub-now-disco,
separate management from beer
garden next door (see separate
write-up), mixed crowd.

## P1

Prinzregentenstraße, Haus der
Kunst (Munich 2)
Tel:  294-252  Hours:  9:30 p.m.-4
a.m., closed Mondays.  Upscale
and dressed up, one of the city's
best nightclubs, bring money.

## Philoma Bar

Schleißheimer Straße 12
(Munich 2)
Tel:  521-319
Hours:  2 p.m.-2 a.m.
(3 a.m. Saturdays)
Variety disco, mixed crowd,
 young and older.

## Regina's Cocktail Lounge

Maximilianstrasse 5  (Munich 2)
Tel:  557-003
Hours:  5 p.m.-3 a.m. (Sun. & Hols.
7 p.m.-3 a.m.)
English pub-style,
conversation and contact.

## Schumann's

Maximilianstraße 36  (Munich 22)
Tel:  229-060
Hours:  6 p.m.-3 a.m.,
closed Saturdays
Spin-off of Harry's New York Bar by
Charles Schumann, former bar-
tender there; "In" bar in Munich,
mixed crowd.

## Vibraphon im Hotel Sheraton

Arabellastraße 6  (Munich 81)
Tel:  924-011
Hours:  9 p.m.-4 a.m.,
 closed Sundays
Live dance music, over 30 crowd.

## Wunder Bar

Hochbrückenstraße 3  (Munich 2)
Tel:  295-118
Hours:  6 p.m.-3 a.m.
DJ music, cellar bar, young.

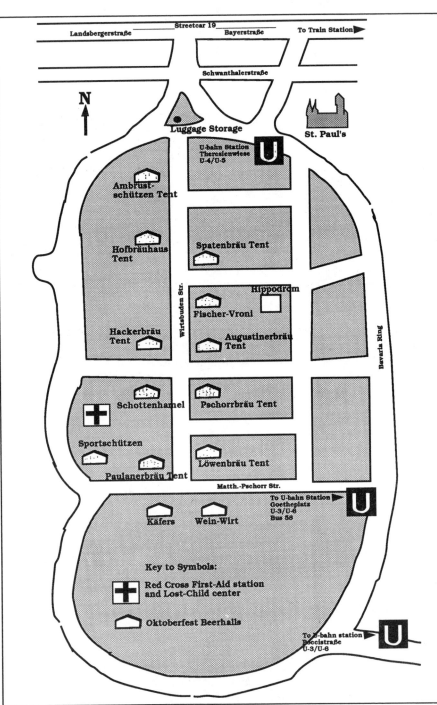

**A map of the Oktoberfest grounds.**
138

# Oktoberfest
## and other Keg Parties

*M*unich loves a party. Münchners look at it this way: There are 365 opportunities on the calendar and none should be wasted. Few are. Every day is a festive occasion in the Bavarian capital. From Christmas and New years and into the strong beer season, through the spring Frühlingsfest and the tri-annual Auer Dults, and finally culminating with Oktoberfest, the year is a collage of one fest after another. Here are the most colorful and enticing of the city's annual offerings.

### Oktoberfest
### (Fall)

This is the grand-daddy of them all, the big beer fest in the sky. It began as a reception for the wedding of Crown Prince Ludwig, later King Ludwig I, to Princess Therese von Sachsen-Hildburghausen, October 12, 1810. What God had joined together, let no man turn asunder, and that included the wedding party. The idea for the royal beer bash is credited to a hackney coachman, Franz Baumgartner. A non-commissioned officer in the Bavarian national guard, Baumgartner suggested spicing up the wedding celebration with a horse race to be run in a meadow just outside of town. His idea won royal approval, and a race track was built in time for Baumgartner to enter and win top prize himself. He rode his horse first

**The Oktoberfest in Munich's Wies'n attracts up to a million people a day.**

139

across the finish line to cheers of thousands of his fellow Münchners, many of whom had bet wisely and heavily on both Baumgartner's ability and his personal familiarity with the track. So huge a triumph in honor of so distinguished a couple called for a victory celebration that lasted through the night and into the next day. Even after the nuptial duo had long departed for the honeymoon, the fest roared on. In fact, the party was such a success the people of Munich insisted it be thrown again the next year. So it was, and so it has been, in the same meadow, named for the bride, *Theresienwiese*, or as the people in Munich say in abbreviated form, *die Wies'n*.

The rest of the world knows it as Oktoberfest, a mad-cap mixture of folklore, festival and frivolity unequaled anywhere else on the globe. The fest has been canceled only 25 times during its run of 180-plus years: 23 times due to wars, twice (1854 and 1873) due to cholera epidemics. Don't let the name mislead you, the 16-day Oktoberfest usually begins the second to last Saturday in September and always ends the first Sunday in October (see Fest Calendar in this section). The tradition of horse racing competition continued for many years, and along with it grew the custom of including a farmer's market and agricultural exhibit. Carnival rides and curious sideshows came later.

The Oktoberfest drew its first 100,000 in 1860, no small feat when you consider that the entire city had only 121,234 population at the time. Beer was there almost from the beginning. By 1890, a number of "beer palaces" were in place and the city's breweries became more and more instrumental in directing the course of the annual festival. By 1900 they had divided the territory up by "tents" and introduced live music and the distinctively Bavarian brass *oom-pah* bands.

The six major Munich breweries sponsor large festival tents (some the size of a multi-story building) as do several private entrepreneurs. Here are names, seating capacities and phone numbers of the largest:

|  |  | ☎ |
|---|---|---|
| Schottenhamel (Spaten) | 8,900 | 592-271 |
| Hackerbräu | 8,300 | 592-374 |
| Hofbräuhaus | 8,100 | 592-467 |
| Pschorrbräu | 8,100 | 532-069 |
| Augustinerbräu | 7,600 | 591-704 |
| Löwenbräu | 7,000 | 532-161 |
| Paulaner-Thomasbräu | 6,800 | 592-591 |
| Ambrustschützenzelt | 6,600 | 591-474 |
| Spatenbräu | 4,200 | 591-906 |
| Schützenzelt | 3,800 | 592-107 |
| Fischer-Vroni | 2,300 | 591-544 |

Each year some 8 million people overwhelm Munich's permanent 1.3 million population and make their way to Oktoberfest. Historically they will down 5 million liters of beer; devour 725,000 roast chickens; inhale 320,000 pairs of grilled sausages; intercept 65,000 pork knuckles; and dismember 72 oxen roasted whole on the spit. Also, at the end of it all, they will take untold number of antacid tablets, flavored bromides and jars of aspirin.

140

A seasonal specialty is the Wies'n Märzen beer, commonly called simply fest or Oktoberfest beer. This is the dark, heavily malted and potent brew that gets its name from centuries ago when religious custom prohibited brewing from April through September. Thus, the dark beer was brewed in March (*März*) to beat the deadline. It was given an especially heavy character that would carry it over until October when it could be properly imbibed. (It was also drunk as soon as it was ready, thus the Starkbierzeit was born. See below.) Now, it might be brewed and dispensed anytime, but during Oktoberfest, it is still a tradition and an alternative to the much more popular *helles* or light (in color) variety.

In addition to the beer, brass bands and the usual armies of buxom mug-toting waitresses, there will be more than 70 carnival rides, including four roller coasters and many others designed with the kids in mind.

Most who visit Oktoberfest have world-class fun and an experience they will never forget. A few will leave disappointed. A trip to Oktoberfest should be made with the realization that this is one of the most crowded 70 acres of real estate anywhere in the world, with up to a million visitors in a single day. With 70,000 seats available in the beer tents, it's hard to imagine no room at the inn, but such is the rule, not the exception. Table reservations can sometimes be had through hotels, tourist offices* or calling the brewery tents themselves. The phone numbers to the tents (listed on previous page) are in operation from early September. Additional phone numbers and Oktoberfest information can be obtained from the Munich visitor bureaus. There are three main visitor bureaus in Munich: at the Marienplatz, the airport, and the main train station. The one at the Hauptbahnhof is the most convenient and is open daily from 8 a.m. to 11 p.m. ,Tel.: (089) 2391-256/257. You can find it at the Bayerstrasse exit, opposite track 12. The visitor bureau will provide a free English-language brochure that answers most questions about Oktoberfest for that particular year.

Here are some worthwhile tips that will make Oktoberfest the positive and memorable experience it should be:

❑ **Take public transportation.** Never even think about driving. You can't park, and you shouldn't risk driving even after one beer. From the Hauptbahnhof, U-bahn 4 or 5 to Theresienwiese drops you off directly in front of the Oktoberfest grounds, in about five minutes.

❑ **Get there early, preferably on a weekday.** Monday through Saturday, the fest opens at 10 a.m. and an hour earlier on Sundays and holidays. Most beer tents close at 10:45 p.m., but a few stay open to 12:30 a.m. (Hippodrom, Käfer, and Weinwirt). There are no real "slack" times at Oktoberfest, and having someone to share all the fun with is never a problem. Thus, a weekday, say between noon and 4 p.m. is a good time to find an available seat. Once you're settled in, you can stay as long as you like.

❑ **Reconsider bringing young children.** Generally, this is a tough place for kids after 5 p.m. You have trouble keeping track of them in the crush of the crowd. They lose interest and become intimidated by it all. Leave them with a baby-sitter at the hotel and they may thank you for it later.

If you bring them, make sure you've made arrangements in case you get separated (it happens). Instruct them not to panic and to seek out a German policeman. He in turn will take them directly to the Red Cross' lost-child station where scores of children are reunited with their misplaced parents every day.

❑ **Have a reserved hotel room waiting**. Munich hotels during Oktoberfest are often booked a year in advance. If you don't have a room reservation already, expect to stay at least 30 miles out of town. If you're stuck, the best bet is to stand by at a large hotel around 10 to 11 a.m. and hope to get lucky with a cancellation. The hotel accommodations bureau at the Hauptbahnhof can also be of help here.

❑ **Bring money.** Oktoberfest is not cheap. Food, drink and rides will strain the pocket book more than expected. Bring a reserve and don't be surprised if you have to dip into it.

❑ **Don't liberate souvenirs**. Don't even harbor a thought of walking out with one of the glass steins as an Oktoberfest remembrance. They are watching and will be happy to lay a heavy fine on you if you are caught. Each Oktoberfest the city produces a special mug (clay ceramic) with the distinctive thematic design for that particular year. It is sold at numerous souvenir kiosks throughout the festgrounds and makes an excellent memento as well as a good investment.

❑ **There's always next year**. If you absolutely can't get to Munich during Oktoberfest, don't fret over it. That only leaves 349 more festive days to choose from. In Munich, every day is Oktoberfest somewhere.

*Beginning September, here are telephone numbers of several tourist offices or ticket outlets that may have seat reservations available. All are in the 089 area code for Munich: Münchner Verkehrsverein-Festring (260-8134); Theaterkasse (120-4421/422); Hieber-Kartenverkauf (226-571); Veranstaltungsdienst Mayr (725-8095); Circus Krone (558-166)

## Auer Dult
## (Fall, Spring, Summer)

A festive tradition even older than Oktoberfest is the Auer Dult. For more than 600 years the fest has been staged three times annually: spring, summer and fall. The event has rotated among a number of locations in Munich. However, since 1905 the combination flea market, antique fair and beer fest has found a permanent home at the Mariahilfplatz, in the shadow of Mariahilf Church.

The "Dult", a colloquial root from the original Latin word *indultum* (indulgence), consists of row after row of booths filled with everything from rare, antique books to hand-painted ceramic figurines, to old Munich memorabilia, to plain-but-useful pots and pans. Naturally, there are plenty of carnival rides, a beer tent, and lots of fast-food stands. There's a garage-sale atmosphere here and the diversity of new and second-hand wares is a special treat for those who enjoy a combination shopping spree and scavenger hunt.

The Auer Dult is full of the unexpected and a visitor never knows what curiosity will eventually follow him home. The precise periods of the nine-day (spanning two weekends) Auer Dult vary from year to year. The spring fest begins the last Saturday in April, the summer Dult usually bridges July and August, and the fall event always begins two weeks after Oktoberfest (see Fest Calendar). Exact dates should be confirmed by calling the main visitors bureau in the Hauptbahnhof (089-2391-256/257).

Mariahilfplatz is near the Deutches Museum. The nearest U-bahn stop is Fraunhofer/Klenzestr. (on the U-2 line out of the Hauptbahnhof). Nearby trams are 15/25/27; and buses, 52 and 56.

### Frühlingsfest
### (Spring)

Locals call it the mini-Oktoberfest and for most visitors it is a suitable alternative when a fall visit is out of the question. It's held in the same area (Theresienwiese) as the Oktoberfest at the end of April (see calendar and again confirm exact dates with visitors bureau). The two-week festival is filled with rides and plenty of eats and cold beer. The city's breweries still turn out in a big way for this extravaganza. The crowds are plentiful, yet smaller than the world-renown fest that occurs six months later. Finding an unreserved seat in one of the beer tents is much less an insurmountable undertaking at the Fruhlingsfest, without having to compromise any of the fun. It's a festive reminder that keg parties in Munich are a year-round affair.

**The tri-annual Auer Dult is half fest, half flea market and always features the unexpected.**

143

## Fasching
### (Winter)

It's tough to find an equal, but the nearest comparison to Fasching is Carnival in Rio, or Mardis Gras in New Orleans. Like the other two festivals, Fasching was originally a religious observance, marking the beginning of lent and a final fling at life's more hedonistic pleasures. In other German population centers — Cologne, Mainz and Düsseldorf, in particular — the celebration is centered on the streets, usually culminating with a Rosen Montag parade (the Monday before Ash Wednesday) accompanied by several days of public partying. In Munich, the season is marked by a variety of indoor masquerade balls, hosted by Munich's more lavish beer emporia. Löwenbräu Keller, Salvator Keller, Hofbräuhaus, and Mathäser Bierstadt head that list. Munich's brand of Fasching is rowdy and ribald, and if organized properly, down right bacchanalian.

From January 7 to Shrove Tuesday six weeks later, the weekends are taken up with these costumed cotillions. It's a night of music, dancing and legalized carousing, when the married, engaged and otherwise betrothed become suddenly single again, even if for just a few hours. The wilder the costume for men — and seemingly the skimpier for women — the better. The packed pavilions are a veritable hunting ground for the bold and venturesome and, with identities protected, even the most timid wallflowers will bloom with utter abandoned. No one arriving in Munich during Fasching time should ever leave town a stranger.

A full schedule of Fasching balls is published in all the city's major newspapers and tickets can be secured at the door or through local tourist and booking agencies. Most major department stores sell basic costume paraphernalia during the Fasching season. There is no minimum dress code, and a few cosmetic touches are enough to put one in the mood and in proper style to make a night of it at a Munich Fasching ball*.

*Those interested in more elaborate costumes can rent them for the evening from numerous agencies who specialize in such outfitting during Fasching time. Here are several possibilities: Heiler Kostümhaus, Corneliusstraße 7, Tel: 268-846/851; Dr. Peter Breuer, Hohenzollernstraße 22, Tel: 399-965; Cinyburg Kostümhaus, Lindwurmstraße 16, Tel: 534-412.

## Starkbierzeit
### (Early Spring)

When the snow melts in Munich, the strongest beer begins flowing. The so-called Starkbierzeit, or strong beer time, is generally a two-week period beginning around "Joseph's Day" on the 19th of March. Local beer halls lay on live brass bands and plenty of schmaltz and glitter. Löwenbräu and Salvator Kellers are especially famous for their generous galas thrown during the potent brew season. In addition to their own famous "-ator" strong brews they dispense with a vengeance, they will also schedule a number of special dances, parties and other events.

A customary attraction are stone-lifting and tossing contests when hundreds vie for the title of Munich's strongest man. Spectators are content to have spent the day with Munich's strongest beer, a heavily malted libation, from 6-8 percent (vol.) alcohol. The muscle-straining matches are always accompanied by plenty of festivities, music, great food and lots of home-grown *gemütlichkeit*.

The Starkbierzeit is celebrated by most Munich beer halls. Münchners refer to it as the city's "fifth season". It's a seasonal bridge, just before spring, when the indoor beer establishments are about to give way to Munich's army of beer gardens. When that happens, the party moves out doors until late in the fall.

### Frühschoppen
### (Sunday mornings)

Not exactly a fest, but certainly a custom worth noting, Frühschoppen is the patently Bavarian (Catholic) habit of spending one's late Sunday mornings at the nearest lokal, beer hall or beer garden. The tradition originally began as a sensible diversion for husbands while their wives and family were off in church. Now, the whole family will show around 10 a.m., having already attended an early Mass. Men share war stories, the women talk about the men and their war stories, the children just bored by it all. It takes place over several *Frühschoppen* (literally "early pints") of beer. Something to remember when quiet Sunday mornings seem to break without much potential: the beerhalls and gasthauses just may be full.

## Munich's Fest Calendar

| | 1992 | 1993 | 1994 | 1995 | 1996 |
|---|---|---|---|---|---|
| **Oktoberfest** | Sep 19 -Oct 4 | Sep 18 -Oct 3 | Sep 17 -Oct 2 | Sep 16 -Oct 1 | Sep 21 -Oct 6 |
| **Auer Dult\*** Spring | Apr 25 -May 3 | Apr 24 -May 2 | Apr 30 -May 8 | Apr 29 -May 7 | Apr 27 -May 5 |
| Summer | Jul 25 -Aug 2 | Jul 31 -Aug 8 | Jul 30 -Aug 7 | Jul 29 -Aug 6 | Jul 27 -Aug 4 |
| Fall | Oct 17 -Oct 25 | Oct 16 -Oct 24 | Oct 15 -Oct 23 | Oct 14 -Oct 22 | Oct 19 -Oct 27 |
| **Frühlingsfest\*** | Apr 25 -May 10 | Apr 24 -May 9 | Apr 23 -May 8 | Apr 22 -May 7 | Apr 20 -May 5 |
| **Fasching (Rosen-Montag)** | Mar 2 | Feb 22 | Mar 14 | Feb 27 | Feb 19 |
| **Starkbier-zeit** | Two weeks in March, always encompassing March 19 (St. Joseph's Day). The exact dates are set several months ahead of time. | | | | |

**NOTE:** *Dates for 1993-96 Frühlingsfest and Auer Dults are probable. Precise dates are set a year ahead of time. Confirm with Munich visitor bureau, Tel: (089) 2391-256/257.

# Beer

*B*eer. You may not know much about it, but you know what you like. And if you know Munich's beer, you already like it. There really isn't a whole lot of prior knowledge required to enjoy what's in the glass. But a couple of facts here and there add to the appreciation of Munich's best-known product and enforce its reputation as the world's premier beverage.

### How Strong the Brew?

The short course on German beer begins with a comparison of potencies, because here is an area where confusion abounds. A popular myth ascribes German beer to be something akin to America's "White Lightnin'", a liquid tornado in a Mason jar. For example, foreigners, when asked, will often estimate German beers to be two or three times the potency of their American, Canadian, or British liquid counterparts. The beer's heavy hops and malt content supports the illusion when a slightly bitter taste is mistaken for a higher alcohol content.

Adding to the confusion is the lack of international standards in measuring alcohol content of beers. For example, America normally measures content by weight, Canada by volume, and Britain by gravity. Thus, a "light beer" in Milwaukee would have 3.2 percent alcohol by weight (the infamous "three-two" beer of one's youth). But the same beer in Ottawa would measure 4 percent volume, and 1030 gravity in London (nobody really knows what that number means). The preferred common denominator is to measure the alcohol content as a percentage of volume, as it is on the label of most German beers. So, for purposes of comparison, alcohol contents of beers mentioned in this book are measured by volume. In the mishmash of conflicting data, it's a good yardstick to use.

Using that standard, most German brews, and 90 percent of those served in Munich, contain about 4.5-5 percent alcohol by volume, only slightly stronger than regular American and British beers ("bitters") that run around 4.4 percent. Not exactly the potent, fiery brew of popular mythology. Where the legend lingers is in the one-liter-fits-all approach to dispensing beer. In the typical Munich beer hall or beer garden, one orders a liter or nothing at all. Sometimes, in a restaurant or before 2 p.m. in the afternoon, half-liters are served. But normally it's the full ration, and any brew would seem industrial-strength when consumed in such quantities. Interestingly, only in Munich and a few other Bavarian cities are the compulsory beer servings so large. In the rest of Germany, the normal glass of beer is 3- to 4-tenths of a liter, or 10-13 ounces.

Not that there aren't strong German brews. There are some, but they are dispensed sparingly, and usually on special occasions. The best-known of the muscle beers are bock and dopplebock. Bock beers — also known as Maibock, Märzen or Oktoberfest beer — run a higher potency level of 5-6.5 percent. The highly concentrated Dopplebocks are a German beer-drinking secret weapon. They are most popular during Starkbierzeit, the strong beer season running from mid- to late March. Dopplebock beers run 7-8 percent alcohol and should be handled with care.

### Why does it taste so good?
Although some have to acquire the taste, the most discriminating beer-drinker is usually won over to German beer with the first smooth and frothy gulp. The beer is just that good. Why? Two reasons: freshness and purity. The first attribute is due to the stubbornness of most German brewers to give in to the all-too-common industrial practice of pasteurization. The process, most often employed to sanitize raw milk products, requires hyper-heating the liquid long enough to kill all the bacteria. The treated beverage can then be shipped across long distances and remain stable, making it practical for overseas markets. However, the longevity of the brew comes at a high price. "Authentic" German beers exported in this manner lose their distinctive qualities, since the pasteurization and use of preservatives give them an acrid, excessively bitter and "skunky" taste.

And why pasteurize anyway? In Germany, where even the smallest village has its own brewery, "shipping" beer usually means delivering several kegs to the gasthaus or beer garden around the corner. Product equilibrium, when demand is matched by production, lets the brewer avoid having to resort to any manufacturing slight of hand to extend shelf life. Certainly, he would rather pour the beer down the drain than do anything that might alter the taste. As if that weren't enough, the integrity of the brew is further protected by a centuries old German law.

In 1516, Bavarian Duke Wilhelm IV decreed the world's oldest food purity law, the German *Reinheitsgebots*. A careful reading of the law reveals it was primarily concerned with fixing beer prices, a nagging public issue throughout German history. Yet, one small "rider" in the original royal ruling has had its impact over the centuries. It stipulated that beer will only consist of four ingredients: yeast, hops, barley malt and water. Of course, in 1516, that's about all there was, so it was no radical pronouncement. But while the price of beer has continued to rise over the centuries, the four-ingredient limit has not. To this day the purity law is in force, not just in Bavaria, but in most of Germany. It will soon be implemented in former East Germany now that reunification has taken place. No chemicals, no preservatives, no sugars that don't occur naturally, no corn syrups or other sweeteners, and no substitute grains — just the four basic ingredients. (Special beers, such as Weizen or wheat beer, are allowed to be manufactured using alternative grains.) If there is any secret to the palate-pleasing quality of German beer, it is embodied in this iron-clad law. It makes all the more impressive the ingenuity and creativity of German brewers who comply with the law and still produce distinctive, high quality beverages. It is both their trial and their salvation.

The purity law has been challenged on numerous occasions as making it almost impossible to compete in overseas markets. Thus, for export, the law has been relaxed, to the detriment of the product sold for foreign consumption. Yet, within Germany the law has been zealously guarded and each attempt to overturn it has been soundly rebuked by the German beer-drinking public.

As the beer brewing science has held fast to its four basic ingredients, the number of its practitioners has diminished. In 1790, Munich had 60 breweries. In 1819, stiff competition reduced the number to 35. By 1865 only 15 remained. Today, the "big six" dominate the Munich brewing scene: Augustinerbräu, Hacker-Pschorrbräu, Hofbräuhaus, Löwenbräu, Paulaner-Thomasbräu, Spatenbräu. Combined, they employ some 4,000 people in the production of 135 million gallons of beer annually. Smaller breweries with avid followings if not huge distributorships include Ayingerbräu, Schneider, Forschungsbrauerei, and Weihenstephan.

### "Gimmeabeer"

Ask simply for a beer in Munich and you will get a *Helles*, or pale-colored lager beer. It will have a heavy head of foam and come in a one-liter glass mug. It will have an aromatic, sweet, malty taste and be less bitter than other German beers. It will be cold, filling and thirst-quenching. Dieters take note that it will contain the equivalent of 400 calories, less than milk or most fruit juices. It will be a popular style of a particular type of beer that draws its distinctive characteristics from the way it is brewed.

In Munich or elsewhere, there are basically two categories of beer: bottom-brewed and top brewed. This refers to beers where the yeast rises to the top, or settles to the bottom, during the fermentation process. Historically, the top brewing method came first. The biggest problem with this style of brewing was the instability of the beer. It would go bad quickly if it were not kept in a cold place. Thus, brewing was somewhat seasonal, with most

duction occurring during the winter and spring months. Then the brew
s stored in cold cellars or alpine caves, in sufficient quantities to last
ough the hot and thirsty summer and fall months. In essence, this is how
: *bierkeller* was born. The celler was where the beer was kept; the garden
ere it was sold and drunk. Somehow the two have become interchangeable
d a bierkeller in Munich is likely a beer garden whether or not there is a
lar on the premises. Shade-bearing chestnut trees were added to keep
: cellar that much cooler and the tradition has stuck.

While the beer was stored for long periods in a cold environment,
servers noted that after the yeast settled to the bottom the brew would
:p indefinitely. Eventually a method was devised in Pilsen (today
:choslovakia) and Vienna to brew the beer from the beginning with the
ist on the bottom. Pilsener and Lager (from the German word *Lager*, to
re) beers were developed in this way and today they dominate the German
d majority of the European) beer market.

A good lager beer is stored for between one and three months while it
itures. The lagering is carried out at about 32-36 degrees Fahrenheit. The
ult is a clean-tasting, golden colored, thirst-quenching brew that abounds
Germany and in most beer-drinking countries around the globe. It's the
st popular of all brews and the one you'll get if you simply ask for a beer
ywhere in Munich.

### A Spectrum of Beers
Among the bottom-brewed Munich beers in evidence, besides the
lles variety served everywhere, are the Pilsener, Dunkeles, Bock,
ppelbock, and so-called Diät Pils and Leicht beers.

### Pilsener
The Pilsener, or "Pils", is a type of lager that is similar in color and
:ture to the helles style, but slightly more bitter due to the higher amount
iops used for flavoring. Pils is by far the most popular beer in central and
:thern Germany. In Munich it is less frequently served and is primarily
ind in special "Pilsbars" that often resemble small, corner neighborhood
bs. The secret of a proper Pils, always with its distinctive whipped-cream
id and served in a thin-stemmed wide-mouthed glass, is the time it takes
pour it. The process consists of filling a glass with 90 percent foam and
n waiting patiently for the suds to turn to golden beer. Then more foam
poured in, followed by more waiting. Finally, when ready, the beer is
ved with a small circular paper doily laced around the base. German Pils
ers will tell you it takes a full seven minutes to pour one properly. It's one
son first-time Pils drinkers are certain the bartending crew has gone on
:ak and totally forgotten their order. Pilseners run about 5 percent alcohol
volume. Although Pils is king of beers in other German regions,
unchner-style-beer lovers who venture forth can still have their *helles* and
nk it too by ordering an "export". Unfortunately, export in this case has

149

nothing to do with it being available outside the country, but it is essentially the same beer served down south in Munich.

### Dunkeles (dark Münchner)

Dunkeles, or "dark" beer, also comes served in a one-liter glass mug and is a function of taste. It is still basically a lager, bottom-brewed beer, but with a higher concentration of malt. The burnt malt used in the brewing process gives it its dark brown color (it resembles a cola soft drink). Outside the city, it is often referred to as a Münchner. Despite its heavy color, it is relatively weak, running around 4.3 percent alcohol.

### Bock Beer

Outside of Germany, "bock" is a term often mistakenly used to refer to any and all dark beers, such as the Münchner style mentioned above. Within the country, especially in Munich, it is the general term for a strong beer, usually pale in color like a helles (there is a dark variety as well), that runs around 6-7 percent alcohol. The name is derived from its city of origin, Einbeck, in Lower Saxony. Since "bock" means billy-goat in German, it is commonly associated in commercial advertising with the symbol of the goat, and the astrological sign of Capricorn. Bock beer is a staple brew during those special festive occasions, such as the March Starkbierzeit and the fall Oktoberfest. Bock beer is strong. Doppelbock is stronger still.

### Doppelbock

High-calibered and potent, doppelbock beer is the most formidable of Munich's beer arsenal. Approaching a barley wine in its consistency and punch, doppelbock was first brewed by the Paulaner brewery and marketed as its world-famous Salvator brand. The -ator suffix has been adopted by every super-strength beer in Munich (see section on Salvator Keller). Doppelbock is the liquid fuel for the city's strong beer craziness days. The high alcohol content — a minimum of 7.5 percent and usually more — dominates the taste of this brew. The strongest of the strain is *eisbock*, alluding to the method used in concentrating the alcohol. The beer is reduced in temperature to below freezing. Since alcohol freezes at a lower temperature than water, the liquid that is siphoned off is much higher in alcohol than occurs naturally during the fermentation process. The synthetically high 13 percent alcohol content of eisbock puts it in a league with distilled spirits. A shot of *schnapps* will do essentially the same job.

### Diät Pils

This is a low-salt and low-carbohydrate beer for diabetics. It has little to do with weight reduction. The closest foreign equivalent to this style of beer are the so-called "dry" beers that are currently popular in the United States. The 6 percent alcohol content of Diät Pils makes it higher in both potency and calories than regular Pils.

### Leicht Beers

Taking the lead from marketing successes in fitness-conscious America, several Munich breweries have begun producing *leicht* or "light" versions of their most popular helles beers. Paulaner, Spaten, and Ayinger currently market reduced-alcohol (about 3.5 percent) beers that retain most of the taste but "40 percent less calories and alcohol" than their regular beers. The lower-octane brews are catching on quickly, and the trend will likely lead to all the city's major breweries following suit. Löwenbräu sells an especially taste-worthy non-alcoholic (0.5 percent or less) beer that can be drunk as is or mixed with a regular beer as a "spacer" to help deal with the high-volume tendency of Munich's beer-dispensing industry.

Top-brewed beers in Munich come in three types, Alt, Kölsch, and Weizen.

### Alt

Alt is the German answer to British ale. The name refers to the old-style brewing practice that gives this beer a bitter, hop-accentuated taste. Copper colored and far less carbonated than common lagers, alt is not nearly as popular in Munich as it is up north. This brew is an unusual style for Bavaria that appeals to a small but devoted following among the city's beer drinkers. The beer is slightly weak, with about a 3.5-4 percent alcohol content.

### Kölsch

Kölsch is a Munich import. The characteristic beer of Cologne (Köln in German) from which it derives its name, Kölsch is a lightly carbonated, almost flat, beer that is extremely pale in color. The beer usually runs about 4.6 percent alcohol, and has a mild, lactic taste.

### Weizen, Weiss

Weizen, or wheat, beer is the most popular non-lager beer in Munich, probably in Germany. Weizen, often called *Weiss* (white) beer, is a favorite on hot days when it is consumed with a slice of lemon in its special half-liter, tall, vase-shaped glass. The amber-colored beer is highly carbonated and its wheat base gives it a light, dry quality that makes it especially popular as a summer refreshment. At upward of 6 percent alcohol, its hidden potency will sneak up on the unsuspecting beer drinker. When Weizen beer is mixed half-and-half with lemon-lime soda, it's called *Russiches* and is available at a few of Munich's larger beer gardens (Chinesischer Turm, for example).

# Lists

**Weekend Variety Pack (limited-time itinerary)**
**Day One:** Waldwirtschaft Großhesselohe
Augustiner Keller
Hofbräuhaus
**Day Two:** Hirschgarten
Chinesischer Turm/Seehaus
Salvator Keller

**Top Baker's Dozen:**
Augustiner Keller
Sankt Emmerams Mühle
Hofbräuhaus
Waldwirtschaft Großhesselohe
Hirschgarten
Seehaus
Michaeligarten
Brückenwirt
Chinesischer Turm
Hinterbrühl
Mangostin-Asia
Menterschwaige
Kloster Andechs

**Cheapest:**
Deutsche Eiche
Hirschgarten
Kloster Andechs
Leiberheim
Menterschwaige
Schießstätte
Tannengarten
Weihenstephen

**Biggest:**
Hirschgarten
Augustiner Keller
Chinesischer Turm
Mathäser Bierstadt
Leiberheim
Kloster Andechs
Löwenbräu Keller

**(Biggest - Cont.)**
Salvator Keller
Waldwirtschaft Großhesselohe
Schießstätte


**Closest (10-minutes or less
walk from Bahnhof):**
Park Cafe
Augustiner Keller
Mathäser Bierstadt
Viktualienmarkt
Augustiner Großgastätte
Hofbräuhaus


**Best with Kids:**
Am Hopfengarten
Augustiner Keller
Hirschgarten
Menterschwaige
Michaeligarten
Seehaus
Siebenbrunn
Waldwirtschaft Großhesselohe

**Under-30 Crowd:**
Chinesischer Turm
Haus der 111 Biere
Hirschau
Max-Emanuel Brauerei
Park Cafe

**Wild-and-Craziest:**
Hofbräuhaus
Mathäser Bierstadt
Salvator Keller
Chinesischer Turm
Waldwirtschaft Großhesselohe


**Most Traditional:**
Augustiner Großgastätte
Hofbräuhaus
Hinterbrühl

Sankt Emmerams Mühle
Zum Flaucher
Menterschwaige
Hirschgarten

## Foul-Weather Picks:
Hofbräuhaus
Augustiner Großgastätte
Mathäser Bierstadt
Salvator Keller
Löwenbräu Keller
Altes Hackerhaus
Haus der 111 Biere
Max-Emanuel Brauerei
Weisses Bräuhaus

## Brewed on the Premises:
Forschungsbrauerei
Weihenstephan
Kloster Andechs
Löwenbräu Keller
Salvator Keller

## Best-tasting Beer:
Augustiner
Paulaner
Forschungsbrauerei's
   *Pilsissimus*
Ayinger
Hofbräuhaus

**A day at the Oktoberfest, 1907.**

# Glossary

**Bayerischer Abend** - Literally "Bavarian evening" , a traditional folk theater program of music, folk dancing, skits and unintelligible humor.

**Beergärtler** - Those who consider the enjoyment of Munich's beer gardens to be a modern science.

**Blasmusik** - Rousing folk music, played by a brass band, often featured in Munich's beer halls. Great to drink beer by.

**Bräustuberl** - Usually a bar within a restaurant or larger complex. Much like a lokal.

**Flöß** - Party rafting. About 60-70 beer lovers hire a raft, a bar and a band for an afternoon float down the Isar River. Viewed at Brückenwirt, Hinterbrühl beer gardens.

**Gasthaus, Gaststätte, Gasthof, Raststätte, Wirtschaft** - A restaurant and/or beer garden complex. All used interchangeably.

**Gemütlichkeit** - No real English translation, it means warm atmosphere, tradition and hospitality all wrapped up in a single word.

**Glühwein** - Hot, cinnamon-spiced wine. Usually served in winter or on cold evenings.

**Keller** - Literally a "cellar", but usually refers to a beer garden.

**Kneipe** - Another name for a lokal; usually a small, neighborhood establishment.

**Kruge** - German word for beer mug (stein means a rock). "Die Kruge hoch!" is the call to raise mugs for a *prosit*, or toast.

**Lederhosen** - Traditional Bavarian-style suspendered leather (originally deerskin) shorts. Don't wear them unless you're a native.

**Lokal** - (Pronounced "low-cal") A bar or a pub that caters to a loyal clientele.

**Maß** - A liter of beer, usually light or "helles" unless you stipulate something else.

**Oom-pah band** - Bavarian brass band (plays Blasmusik); standard musical program in most beer halls and some beer gardens.

**Radler** - Half beer and half lemon-lime soda. Termed a *radler* (bicyclist) because they're a favorite of bike riders who must navigate their way home.

**Russe** - Half Weissbier (*weizen* or wheat beer) and lemon-lime soda.

**Schmankerl** - Bavarian fast-food. Lots of sausages, roasted chickens, salads and cream-cheeses. Typical beer garden fare — marginally nutritious, heavy starches high in carbohydrates. Naturally, it's delicious.

**Selbstbedienung** - Self service. Sometimes abbreviated SB. Tables without tablecloths usually mean you can bring your own food and serve yourself to the beer.

**Spätze** - Half coca-cola and half orange soda. Kids and women love it.

**Stammtisch** - A table set aside for regulars. If you're not sure whether you're a regular, you're not.

**Wirt** - The proprietor of the business. The boss.